Making a Reality of Community Care

A Report by the Audit Commission

December 1986

LONDON: HER MAJESTY'S STATIONERY OFFICE

Summary

Every year, some £6 billion is spent from public funds providing long-term care and support for elderly, mentally ill or mentally or physically handicapped people excluding the cost of acute hospital care and GP services. About 1.5 million adults in England and Wales receive some form of care ranging from an hour or two of home help each week up to a full range of long-term care 24 hours a day. Of these, one million are elderly (aged over 65); and half a million are younger people who are either mentally or physically handicapped or who require long term support following mental illness.

These clients are cared for in a wide range of settings, from their own homes to a National Health Service (NHS) hospital. Broadly, services can be considered as part of a 'spectrum' of care; for example Exhibit 1 illustrates some of the alternative forms of accommodation available to mentally handicapped people away from the family home and typical total public sector costs (£ per week) in each case:

Exhibit 1

SPECTRUM OF CARE SETTINGS

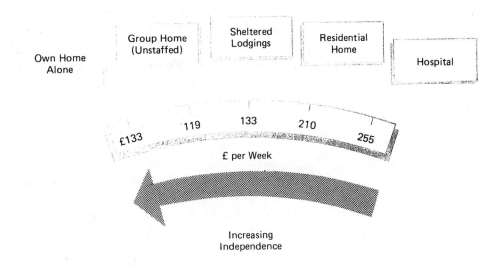

Own Home Alone

Group Home (Unstaffed)

Sheltered Lodgings

Residential Home

Hospital

£133   119   133   210   255

£ per Week

Increasing
Independence

The policy of successive governments has been to promote community-based services allowing the reduction of long-stay hospital provision. This is generally considered better in most situations. It is also more economical in many cases: a frail elderly person living in their own home with day and domiciliary support would typically cost public funds some £135 per week; the same person would cost about £295 per week in a NHS geriatric ward. At the same time, there will always remain a very important role for hospitals (although on a reduced scale) in caring for a small number of very severely handicapped people; and residential care will continue to play an important role in the spectrum of care. 'Community Care' is about changing the balance of services and finding the most suitable placement for people from a wide range of options. It is not about imposing a community solution as the only option, in the way that institutional care has been the only option for many people in the past.

Although there has been worthwhile progress in some areas, and most authorities have at least made a start, care in the community is far from being a reality in many places:

(a) Progress with the build-up of community-based services has generally been slow, and in some places is not keeping pace with the run-down of long-stay institutions in the NHS. Progress has been slowest for mentally ill people: there are over 25,000 fewer hospital beds than there were ten years ago, but community facilities have not kept pace with only an additional 9,000 day care places for example; and no one knows what happens to many people after they are discharged

(b) A very uneven pattern of local authority services has developed, with the care that people receive as much dependent on where they live as on what they need. In well over half of local authorities (LAs), expenditure on services for mentally ill people is less than £1 per head of population, even though one in ten people each year consult their general practitioner about a mental health problem, and one in a hundred is referred to the specialist psychiatric services; and there has for years been general recognition of the significance of the social and environmental aspects of mental illness

(c) Over 300,000 people still live in residential settings. The reduction in NHS facilities has been offset by the growth in private residential homes where some residents are entitled to receive help with their fees from Supplementary Benefits. In 1984 some 40,000 residents were receiving such help at a cost of some £200 million; but the Commission estimates that the cost is now £500 million a year and growing rapidly.

At best, there seems to be a shift from one pattern of residential care based on hospitals to an alternative supported in many cases by Supplementary Benefit payments – missing out more flexible and cost-effective forms of community care altogether. At worst, the shortfall in services will grow, with many vulnerable and disabled people left without care and at serious personal risk.

Although more money could always be spent to advantage, the current levels of expenditure from public funds could provide a community-based service for elderly, mentally ill and handicapped people. But some underlying problems must be tackled first:

– While the Government's policies require a shift from hospital-based (health) services to locally-based (local authority and health) services, the mechanisms for achieving a parallel shift in funds are inadequate. In fact, expenditure on NHS mental illness and mental handicap in-patient services has actually increased, by almost £100 million a year (in 1984–5 prices) since 1976

– Meanwhile, local authorities are often penalised through the grant system for building the very community services which government policy favours and which are necessary if the NHS is to be in a position to close its large long-stay psychiatric hospitals and release the capital assets – conservatively valued at over £500 million

– The funds being made available to bridge the transition phase are limited. For example, NHS revenue expenditure on joint finance and 'dowries' for patients transferred to local authorities is currently about £100 million a year (out of a total NHS expenditure on services for these clients of some £3 billion a year)

- Supplementary Benefit policies fund private residential care more readily than community-based care of which there is still relatively little in the private sector. Partly as a result, private and voluntary homes are expanding very rapidly, particularly on the South Coast – there are now nearly ten times as many places **per 1,000 people aged 75 or over** in private and voluntary residential homes for elderly people in Devon and East Sussex than there are in Cleveland, for example
- While central government attempts to achieve equitable distribution of public funds across the country, through the use of complex formulae both within the NHS and local government, the effects can be largely offset by Supplementary Benefit payments for board and lodgings. If all residents now in local authority care or NHS geriatric and mental health hospitals were to be transferred to private residential care, (an unlikely eventuality – but a useful illustration of the forces at work) Supplementary Benefit payments for board and lodgings would increase up to a theoretical upper limit of more than £2 billion a year
- Responsibility for introducing and operating community-based services is fragmented between a number of different agencies with different priorities, styles, structures and budgets who must 'request' co-operation from each other. For community care to operate these agencies must work together. But there are many reasons why they do not, including the lack of positive incentives, bureaucratic barriers, perceived threats to jobs and professional standing, and the time required for interminable meetings (joint planning alone could easily be occupying the equivalent of 30 professional staff full-time in a large county)
- Staffing arrangements are inadequate. A new impetus in training and a different approach to manpower planning are required. The future of staff in institutions which have a limited life is not clear in many cases; as a result, staff anxiety is high. At the same time, inadequate provision is being made to train staff for community care.

It is therefore not surprising that joint planning and community care policies are in some disarray. The result is poor value for money. Too many people are cared for in settings costing over £200 a week when they would receive more appropriate care in the community at a total cost to public funds of £100 – 130 a week. Conversely, people in the community may not be getting the support they need.

However, in spite of the many obstacles, effective community care is being promoted in a number of authorities. Successful schemes often include the following features: strong and committed local 'champions' of change; a focus on action, not on bureaucratic machinery; locally-integrated services, cutting across agency boundaries; a focus on the local neighbourhood; a multi-disciplinary team approach; and partnership between statutory and voluntary organisations. These successes point the way ahead.

Specifically, the Commission believes that the following actions are required:

(i) A rationalisation of funding policies must be undertaken from the centre so that the present policy conflicts are resolved and the block grant disincentives to the build-up of local authority community care services removed.

(ii) Adequate short-term funding must be provided to avoid the long-term waste of two inadequate services struggling along in parallel indefinitely.

(iii) Social security policies must be co-ordinated with community care policies, and present conflicts and 'perverse incentives' encouraging residential rather than community care removed.

(iv) A more rational organisational structure must be established; local responsibility, authority and accountability for delivering a balanced community-based care service for different client groups need to be more clearly defined.

(v) The organisational structures of the different agencies need to be aligned and greater managerial authority delegated to the local level.

(vi) Staffing arrangements must ensure provision of an appropriate supply of properly trained community-based staff.

(vii) Provision for cost-effective voluntary organisations must be sufficient to prevent them being starved of funds for reasons unrelated to their potential contribution to the support of clients and those caring for them in the community.

The objective of any changes should be to create an environment in which locally integrated community care can flourish – because it is at this level that community care works. Such changes will require some adjustment to the organisational framework for community care. In order to establish how best to achieve this end, a high level review of the current situation should be set in train. The review will need to examine a range of possibilities.

For example, local authorities could be made responsible for the long-term care where required of **mentally and physically handicapped people** in the community except for the most severely disabled who require medical supervision, and the resources necessary to do this could be transferred from the NHS. Where necessary, authorities would buy-in specialised care from the NHS or the private sector.

For long-term care of **elderly people** in the community, a single budget in an area could be established with contributions from the NHS and local authorities; the amount to be determined in each case by a formula agreed centrally. This budget could be under the control of a single manager who would purchase, from whichever public or private agency seems appropriate, services for elderly people in the areas for which he or she is responsible. The manager could report to a small joint board comprising representatives of the bodies with statutory responsibilities in this area.

For **people recovering from mental illness** in the community, the NHS will inevitably remain the prime authority responsible for care; but nevertheless there remains an important role for social services. Two alternatives should be evaluated:

– Assigning to the NHS responsibility for all services; but when services are required from local authorities, these should be purchased, with the local authority acting as contractor

– Setting up an arrangement similar to that proposed above for services for elderly people.

In each case, care funded by social security in the private and voluntary sector should be co-ordinated with care provided by social services and the NHS. This is the subject of a joint DHSS/Local Authority Associations working party.

The one option that is not tenable is to do nothing about present financial, organisational and staffing arrangements. Redeployment of the assets released by the rundown of long-stay hospitals, combined with the projected increase of 37% in the number of very elderly people over the next ten years presents a 'window' of opportunity to establish an effective community-based service to provide the care needed for frail elderly, mentally ill, mentally handicapped and physically handicapped people. If this opportunity is not taken, a new pattern of care will emerge, based on private residential homes rather than a more flexible mix of services which includes residential care where appropriate. The result will be a continued waste of scarce resources and, worse still, care and support that is either lacking entirely, or inappropriate to the needs of some of the most disadvantaged members of society and the relatives who seek to care for them.

Introduction

1. Nearly everybody at some stage of life is incapacitated to some degree by illness or accident. For most people, such periods are relatively short, possibly requiring a stay in hospital followed by a period of recuperation at home before a return to 'normal' life. But for many people, the period of incapacity is anything but short. It may last the rest of their lives; and for some people it may even occupy the whole of their lives. The form of the incapacity may be physical with impaired mobility, sight or hearing; or it may take the form of mental illness or mental handicap; or it may even involve a combination, leaving the person 'multiply-handicapped'. People with such incapacities are usually divided into four 'client groups': elderly, mentally handicapped, mentally ill and physically handicapped people. The principal agencies engaged in caring for these client groups are the National Health Service (NHS), local authorities (housing, personal social services and education) and independent agencies in the private and the voluntary sectors.

2. The majority of people requiring long-term care has always been looked after in the community by their relatives. But for the past hundred years or so, the main way of caring for many of the most disabled members of these client groups has been to accommodate them in an institution. Many such institutions are large, remote and impersonal; and over the last 50 years there has been an increasing trend to seek alternative ways of caring for people in the communities where they and their families have lived. Successive governments have encouraged this trend and have shaped their policies (outlined in Appendix A) to promote the growth of community care services to lend additional support to the majority living in the community, thereby allowing the closure of long-stay institutions and hospitals.

3. These policies relate to a very large number of people. In England and Wales there are 7.5 million elderly people (aged 65 and over) of whom about a million are receiving care; and another half million people under the age of 65 are physically or mentally handicapped. The incidence of mental illness is widespread across the whole community: according to a 1975 White Paper each year some 5 million people consult their general practitioner about a mental health problem with 600,000 of these being referred to the specialist psychiatric services.

4. At any one time over a third of a million people from these client groups are supported through public funds in 'residential care' (hospitals, nursing homes and residential homes). Of these, 210,000 are elderly, 80,000 are mentally ill, 60,000 are mentally handicapped and 10,000 are physically handicapped people aged below 65. These people are accommodated in a variety of settings, supported by the health service (if in hospital), local authorities (either in their own residential accommodation or in private or voluntary accommodation) or by Supplementary Benefits (private or voluntary accommodation) as shown in Table 1:

Table 1: PATTERN OF RESIDENTIAL CARE FUNDED BY THE PUBLIC SECTOR, 1984
Number of Clients

	Elderly	Mentally Ill	Mentally Handicapped (inc. Juniors)	Younger Physically Handicapped	Total
Hospital In-patient	54,100†	70,700	40,600	1,400†	166,800
Local Authority Staffed Homes	109,100	2,400	12,100	5,200	128,800
Private and Voluntary Homes					
– Local Authority Supported*	10,600	1,400	5,000	4,100	21,100
– Supplementary Benefit Supported*	34,900	1,900	2,500	600	39,900
Totals	208,700	76,400	60,200	11,300	356,600

† Elderly and younger physically handicapped in-patient numbers include only those in geriatric beds and in younger disabled units. In addition those client groups occupy beds in other specialties, for example 45% of acute beds are occupied by people over 65.

* The extent of financial support from both LA and supplementary benefits depends on a financial assessment of the client. Figures include those supported by Supplementary Benefits in nursing homes.

The derivation of the numbers in this table and in subsequent tables and exhibits is set out in Appendix B.

5. In addition there are probably in excess of a million people receiving day care or domiciliary care funded through the NHS, social services departments or social security attendance allowances. Three-quarters of these are elderly and the remainder are split between the other client groups, as shown in Table 2:

Table 2: PATTERN OF COMMUNITY CARE FUNDED BY THE PUBLIC SECTOR, 1984
Number of Clients

	Elderly	Other Priority Groups
Day Hospital: daily attendances	7,000	15,000
LA Day Centre/Adult training centre: places	34,000	74,000
Home help: cases/week	453,000	33,000
Meals: recipients/week	218,000	–
Personal Aids: cases/year	302,000	106,000
Attendance Allowances	249,000	177,000

Note: Many people receive combinations of these services but national statistics do not permit any analysis of 'packages of care'.

6. The number of very elderly (aged 75 and over) has increased over the last ten years by 27%; and the number of people aged 85 and over will increase by an estimated 37% over the next ten years as Exhibit 2 shows.

7. The sums of money involved are also very significant, as would be expected given the numbers of people involved. Table 3 shows the distribution of public finance specifically on long-term care at 1984–5 prices – the latest date for which figures are available.

Table 3: EXPENDITURE BY CLIENT GROUP, 1984–5
England: £ million, at out-turn prices

	Elderly	Mentally Handicapped	Mentally Ill	Younger Disabled	Total
National Health Service	£1,060 million	500	1,090	50	2,700
Personal Social Services	1,380	320	60	140	1,900
Social Security	460	30	10	190	690
Total	2,900	850	1,160	380	5,290

Exhibit 2

POPULATION TRENDS 1974-98

England and Wales

Index: 1974 = 100

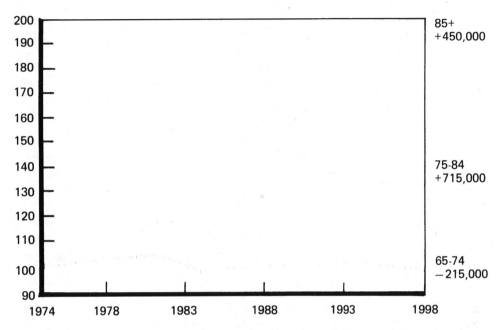

Source: OPCS figures to 1984 and Government Actuary's Department 1983-based forecasts

When Wales is included and these costs are updated to current prices, and trends in social security payments are taken into account, about £6 billion of public finance is directly attributable to care services (as opposed to accommodation or income maintenance, although the 'hotel' costs of institutional care are included):

- The NHS spends about £3 billion (a third of the Hospital and Community Health Services budget) on services specifically for elderly, mentally ill, mentally handicapped and physically handicapped people (with a very large additional sum being spent on acute and primary health care services for these groups: there is a considerable load on GPs, and around 45% of acute beds are occupied by people aged over 65)

- Approximately three-quarters of gross current local authority social services expenditure, amounting to £2 billion a year, is attributable to the same groups

- More than £1 billion a year of social security money is distributed on benefits which contain a specific component for care. A much larger amount is distributed to elderly and disabled people for income support and accommodation.

Of the total of £6 billion, £4 billion is used to provide residential care (hospitals, nursing homes, residential homes).

8. In addition, there is an active voluntary sector which is funded in part from public subscription and provides an invaluable adjunct to public sector services. The role of the voluntary organisation has recently been summarised in '*A Stake in Planning: Joint Planning and the Voluntary Sector*' (ref. 1) recently published by the National Council for Voluntary Organisations as an expert identifier of need, an agent of change and development, a provider of services, a contributor of resources and a vehicle for participation. An increasingly significant private sector, which mainly

consists of private residential and nursing homes – again funded in part from public funds (directly by local authorities and health authorities, or indirectly through residents' entitlement to state benefits) – has also been developing over the last few years offering a wider choice and an alternative to public sector services.

9. Many commentators have observed a danger in using the term 'community care' indiscriminately as a panacea; and that 'community care' policies place an additional burden on relatives at a time when the whole concept of a supporting community is breaking down. As the Government's own White Paper *Growing Older* (ref. 2) states 'care *in* the community must increasingly mean care by the community'. To be sure, the pattern of community support is changing as a recent research report by Willmott for the Policy Studies Institute (ref. 3) reveals:

- Although relatives, particularly women relatives, continue to provide the bulk of care and support – especially personal and domestic care – fewer people than in the past live with or near relatives and local extended families are rare. But contacts with relatives remain at high levels in the form of 'dispersed extended families'; about three-quarters of the adult population see them at least once a week

- Traditional neighbourhoods are in decline. Networks of friends, like those of relatives, are now spread out. But most people have friends who live near their home, and neighbours are mostly friendly and helpful, providing surveillance, auxiliary help and help in an emergency

- Some minorities are socially isolated and others who need continuing care do not receive enough. These include some of the very elderly and in particular confused elderly people, together with families which have mentally handicapped and severely physically handicapped children and adults. Some of the carers of such people, lacking enough outside support are themselves under strain. Moreover, demographic trends are not favourable with growing numbers of very elderly people and fewer children to look after them because of falling family size. Also more married women work, the divorce rate is higher, and changes in women's attitudes towards their roles may make them less willing to provide care for relatives on a long-term basis. Yet there are converse trends, with labour saving devices, more spacious houses, and more leisure time which may to some extent offset the potential reduction in informal care.

10. Given these trends, community care policies must be flexible enough to adopt to changing circumstances. In particular, community care involves:

(a) The development of a wide range of services in a variety of settings providing a wide range of options

(b) The movement of health services out of hospital settings into more local, domestic settings; and a change in balance between the provision of residential care and the provision of day and domiciliary services

(c) The bringing of services to people, rather than people to services; and the adjustment of services to meet the needs of people, rather than the adjustment of people to meet the needs of services

(d) The provision of the minimum amount of intervention necessary to allow people to live their lives as independently as possible; but the provision of sufficient care to ensure effective support.

The change to a community-based service thus involves much more than a change to the pattern of service provision. It involves a change of approach, with emphasis and priority placed on encouraging patients and clients to do as much for themselves as possible (an 'enabling' service), with 'care' provided only where it is really needed. This is because the trend to community care has been taking place in parallel with improvements in ways of helping disabled people to achieve their maximum potential: there have been technical improvements to methods of treatment, drugs, aids and adaptations to property; and possibly most significantly of all there have been improvements to techniques for helping people to acquire or re-acquire many of the basic skills of daily living which can make all the difference to their degree of independence. As a result, severely mentally handicapped people achieve degrees of social competence undreamed of a few years ago; and heavily physically handicapped people can, with sufficient determination and assistance, lead relatively independent lives in their own homes.

11. In practice, enabling and care are two sides of the same coin, as it were. For more seriously handicapped people, care will always be needed; but even the most severely handicapped can be encouraged to live more independently, realising their full potential within a service that combines enabling with caring. To provide the necessary framework for such an approach, a wide range of services that complement each other is required.

12. Services can be considered as part of a 'spectrum' of care ranging from minimal domiciliary care for those with minor difficulties with one or two tasks, to long-stay hospital care for those totally dependent on outside support for nearly all functions. Exhibit 1 showed some of the alternative forms of accommodation available outside the family home for mentally handicapped people. Similar examples can be drawn for the other client groups. People living in the situations illustrated in Exhibit 1 are supported by day care and domiciliary services. For example a resident in 'sheltered' lodgings might be supported by a specially trained landlady, five days a week at a local authority training centre, and support with daily living activities from resettlement and homecare staff (averaging one hour a week, say).

13. The change-over to community care is, therefore, a fundamental shift, not only in the location of services, but also in the type and range of services provided and in organisational attitudes and skills of staff involved. It thus presents a considerable challenge to management. Any failure to meet the challenge of community care will result in a lower quality service and reduced value for money. While the total cost of community care may be comparable with the cost of institutional care, different individual placements have markedly different cost implications as Table 4 shows. The table provides

Table 4: COSTS OF CARE IN DIFFERENT SETTINGS
£ per week, 1986 prices

ILLUSTRATIVE

Care Setting	Example A	Example B
Own Home		
– domiciliary service	£ 97.35 per week	
– as above, plus day care	135.35	132.50
Local Authority		
– sheltered housing	151.55	
– residential (Part III) home	133.25	190.25
Private and Voluntary		
– residential home	138.55	209.55
– nursing home	183.55	
NHS Hospital	294.75	254.75

two examples to illustrate the order-of-magnitude differences in the costs incurred by the public sector as a whole for care in different settings:

- Example A shows the costs for a frail elderly single person on a state pension, without substantial savings. The client qualifies for Attendance Allowance at the lower rate, for a disability incurred after retirement age
- Example B is a mentally handicapped adult with no savings or other income. The client qualifies for Severe Disablement Allowances, but not for Attendance Allowance.

Clearly, the cost of an inappropriate placement is significant. Recent studies and audits have shown that people are placed in residential care who are not as dependent as the person in Example A. Under these circumstances, such people are receiving more care than they need, undermining their independence and increasing costs. At the same time there are people in the community who are receiving insufficient support, possibly putting them at risk. Either way, poor value for money results.

14. Moreover, even where there are no cost advantages because of the level of domiciliary support required, there is general agreement that for most people a higher quality of life can be realised in the community if proper community services are available. Community services are therefore usually more effective, since they meet peoples' needs better; and they are more efficient, since they achieve more for the same amount of money. Achieving maximum value for the £6 billion a year of public expenditure therefore means that effective community care services should be introduced as rapidly as possible.

15. The Government's policies on community care thus have a major effect on the economy, efficiency and effectiveness of local authorities in meeting local needs – and in particular on the personal social services, but also to a lesser extent on education and housing (15% of homeless households accepted for rehousing during 1985 involved people disabled in some way).

16. In the light of these potential effects, the Commission has undertaken a study of developments in the care in the community of adult members of the groups described above, and of the joint planning arrangements for promoting these developments. [Services for children have been excluded to keep the study within manageable proportions although many of the conclusions apply]. The study has been undertaken under section 27 of the *Local Government Finance Act,* of 1982, which requires the Audit Commission to undertake or promote studies designed to 'enable it to prepare reports as to the impact of the operations of any particular statutory provision or provisions or of any directions or guidance given by a Minister of the Crown ... on economy, efficiency and effectiveness in the provision of local authority services or on their financial management'. The study has focused on the following questions:

- To what extent are community care policies being adopted in practice
- To what extent are funding policies helping or hindering local authorities' economy, effectiveness and efficiency
- To what extent are organisational arrangements helping or hindering local authorities economy, effectiveness and efficiency?

Inevitably the study has concentrated on community care from the local authority perspective because of the Commission's specific responsibilities; but it has been necessary to comment on other agencies – particularly health authorities – where they impinge on the economy, effectiveness and efficiency of local authorities.

17. Initial consultations were started in June 1985. A small study team was formed in October 1985 completing its work 12 months later in October 1986. The team consisted of members of the Commission's own staff, Stanley Griffiths, a District Health Authority Treasurer seconded to the Commission for six months and Ian Mackinder, a management consultant. The work has involved a review of the extensive literature, analysis of national data, and fieldwork in a cross-section of local authorities and their equivalent health authorities. The authorities visited formed a sample of the population stratified by type of authority, geographical location and whether or not their boundaries coincided, and served in total 8% of the population of England and Wales. A number of Regional Health Authorities (RHAs) were also visited. During the fieldwork, the issues were discussed with senior staff and details of innovative community-based schemes were obtained. A survey of local authorities was also mounted to monitor recent trends in the registration of private and voluntary homes, and numbers of people being financially supported by local authorities. Following completion of the current study, the Commission intends to follow up in more detail many of the key issues in a special study of local authority services for mentally ill and mentally handicapped people. The study team would like to acknowledge the considerable help and support of the many people from health and local authorities who have met members of the team during this study. In particular, a group of advisors has provided considerable experience and valuable guidance as the study has proceeded. Notwithstanding all the consultation and assistance, as with all its reports, responsibility for the conclusions rest with the Commission alone.

18. The report that follows summarises, in turn, the Commission's main conclusions:

(i) *There are serious grounds for concern* about the lack of progress in shifting the balance of services towards community care. Progress has been slow and uneven across the country; and the near-term prospects are not promising. In short, the community care policy is in danger of failing to achieve its potential. Chapter 1 describes the evidence for the Commission's concerns in more detail.

(ii) *Fundamental underlying problems need to be tackled,* if community care is to be translated from an attractive policy to reality throughout England and Wales. In chapter 2, the major underlying problems are discussed:

- The pattern of distribution of finance is out of step with community care policies. Local authorities cannot be expected to play their full part given the loss of grant incurred for expanding services under current arrangements

- There is considerable organisational fragmentation and confusion, with responsibility for the introduction of community care divided between a variety of separately funded organisations who often fail to work together effectively

- There are inadequate arrangements for training and providing opportunities in community services for existing staff in long-stay hospitals, and for training sufficient numbers of community-based staff.

(iii) *Radical steps will be necessary* if the underlying problems are to be solved. Fine-tuning the existing arrangements, or treating the symptoms, will not meet the needs of the situation. In chapter 3, various ways of tackling the problems are considered. In spite of the difficulties outlined above, progress is being made and a number of good examples are given. Such progress can usually be attributed to individuals with enough determination to manoeuvre their way around the system; they are succeeding in spite of, not because of, the present organisation and financing arrangements. Such a situation is clearly less than satisfactory if community care is to become a local reality everywhere.

The final chapter also sets out the Commission's proposals for the way forward – recognising that at this stage the Commission is not in a position to put forward specific recommendations for action. The purpose of this report is to convince all the interests concerned that at present, community care is far from a reality for many of the very people it is intended to help.

1. Grounds for Concern

19. During 1981 the Government stated in *Care in Action* (ref. 4) that 'it has been a major policy objective for many years to foster and develop community care for the main client groups – elderly, mentally ill, mentally handicapped and disabled people and children – as well as for the special and smaller groups such as alcoholics'. The study has sought evidence of the extent of the change in the balance of care; there should be an increasing proportion of people cared for by domiciliary and day care services in their own homes with a corresponding reduction in institutional services.

20. Unfortunately, however, progress towards community care has been slow. Analysis suggests that:

   (i) Progress has been generally slower than would be needed to offset the rundown in NHS provision.

   (ii) The response across the country has been very uneven: the situation in some areas is much more serious than the national figures would suggest.

   (iii) Future prospects are unattractive.

The rest of this chapter deals in detail with each of these conclusions in turn.

SLOW PROGRESS

21. The White Papers outlining policies for services for mentally handicapped and mentally ill people required a shift in the pattern of service delivery from large hospitals to community based services, and from health to social services. Since the situation differs between groups of clients, it makes sense to consider the main conclusions separately:

   (i) Progress towards targets for services for mentally handicapped people set as long ago as 1971 has been slow. Since 1971 'best practice' has advanced so that the 1971 targets are now out of date, leaving many authorities even further behind.

   (ii) The situation is even less satisfactory so far as services for mentally ill people are concerned. Progress in reducing NHS hospital provision for this group has been faster than the build-up of community resources.

   (iii) There has been no increase per person aged 75 or over in community-based services central to supporting elderly people: home helps and meals-on-wheels.

Services for Mentally Handicapped People

22. In 1971, the Government published a White Paper entitled *Better Services for the Mentally Handicapped* (ref. 5) which outlined the principles of community care, and provided guidance to local authorities and health authorities on the lines on which the Government wished their services to develop. The paper identified 'a serious shortage of adult training centres, a gross shortage of residential accommodation, and great need for more trained staff of all kinds'. It also identified many shortfalls in the hospital service and as a result outlined a 20-year programme for switching services from the hospitals to the community. Progress towards the targets set out at

that time is shown in Table 5.

Table 5: PROGRESS TO WHITE PAPER TARGETS FOR MENTALLY HANDICAPPED
PEOPLE
England and Wales

	1969	1984	Target (by 1991)	Progress to target
Hospitals (available beds-adults)	52,100	42,500	27,300	39%
Residential Places (local authority, private and voluntary)	4,300	18,500	29,800	56%
Local Authority Adult Training Centre Places	24,600	50,500	74,500	52%

23. For mentally handicapped people the build-up of community services is actually ahead of the run-down of hospital places (although all services are well behind the schedules set by the White Paper). However, since 1971 concepts of what is possible have moved on, making the targets out of date. More recent developments are considerably more radical than some of the proposals put foward in 1971 'moving the goal posts' even further from the institutional service model. Experience gained over the last 20 years has shown that mentally handicapped people are able to live much more independently than was envisaged in 1971. Furthermore, some authorities are moving ahead very well. Hence, others must be doing little or nothing at all for the average progress to be behind even the 1971 schedule. Table 6 shows the current balance of expenditure for services for mentally handicapped people between health and social service, and between community care and residential care (hospital, staffed residential home):

Table 6: BALANCE OF EXPENDITURE FOR MENTALLY HANDICAPPED PEOPLE
England only

	1977	1985	Pattern implied by 1971 White Paper Target
Health	73.8%	64.5	44.2
Social Services	26.2	35.5	55.8
Residential Care	82.3	79.0	66.6
Community Care	17.7	21.0	33.4

The first column shows the situation in 1977. The second shows the situation in 1985 and the third shows the pattern proposed in the 1971 White Paper. The balance proposed for one authority (Plymouth, which is one of the more forward-looking areas described more fully in chapter 3) implies a reduction in health spending to 32.4% and an increase in expenditure on community care to 66%. Other authorities are shifting the balance even further than Plymouth. The conclusion is inescapable: many authorities have a considerable distance yet to travel before community care becomes a local reality for mentally handicapped people. Other commentators have remarked on this slow progress over the years.

Services for Mentally Ill People

24. In 1975 a White Paper *Better Services for the Mentally Ill* (ref. 6) was published, setting a framework for the development of services for mentally ill people. Table 7 shows the progress that has been made towards the White Paper's targets.

Table 7: PROGRESS TO WHITE PAPER TARGETS FOR MENTALLY ILL PEOPLE
England only

	1974	1984	Target	Progress to target
Hospitals (available beds)	104,400	78,900	47,900	45%
Residential Places (local authority, private and voluntary)	3,500	6,800	11,500	41
Day Hospital Places*	11,200	17,000	45,800*	17
Day Centre Places (local authority and voluntary)	5,400	9,000	28,200	16

* The target includes day hospital provision for in-patients. Many in-patients receive day care in hospitals but are not included in the day hospital statistics.

25. The table shows that not only has there been relatively slow progress overall, but the changes are out of balance. While the number of hospital beds has been reduced by 25,000, the community facilities (day hospital and day centre places) have increased by 9,000. The number of community psychiatric nurses has only risen from 1,300 in 1980 to 2,200 in 1984, compared with over 80,000 nurses in mental illness and mental handicap hospitals and units. However, the number of out-patient clinics has been increasing more rapidly since the publication of the White Paper.

26. The elements that go to make up a comprehensive district service broadly remain those set out in the White Paper. The targets imply a shift in expenditure from the NHS to local authorities, and from residential to community care as set out in Table 8 below.

Table 8: BALANCE OF EXPENDITURE FOR MENTALLY ILL PEOPLE
England only

	1977	1985	Pattern implied by 1975 White Paper Target
Health	97.0%	95.5	87.0
Social Services	3.0	4.5	13.0
Residential Care*	90.7	86.2	66.2
Community Care	9.3	13.8	33.8

* Hospital, Nursing Homes, Residential Homes

27. Moreover, clinical advances in the last decade mean that the targets set in 1975 are now out of date. Tables 7 and 8 have measured the progress towards community care as envisaged in the 1975 White Paper. However, many professionals now have more ambitious targets; and a number of authorities have plans that imply a greater change to the pattern of care and to the balance of expenditure. In Torbay (one of the areas described further in chapter 3) the agreed plan implied that expenditure on community care will rise to 44% of the total expenditure on services for mentally ill people, although 93% of this total expenditure will still be incurred by the health authority.

* * *

28. These global figures mask the reality for patients and their families. It must be a matter for grave concern that although there are 37,000 fewer mentally ill and mentally handicapped patients today than there were ten years ago, no one knows what has happened to many of those who have been discharged. Some, of course, have died; others are likely to be in some form of residential care; the rest should be receiving support in the community. But no one has the necessary information to confirm whether or not this is in

fact the case. If recent US experience is any guide, it is likely that a significant proportion of those discharged from NHS hospitals will have been before the Courts and will now be imprisoned; others will have become wanderers, left to their own devices with no support from community-based services.

29. Evidence supports this concern. The second report from the Social Services House of Commons Select Committee (1984–5 session) dealt with community care with special references to adult mentally ill and mentally handicapped people (ref. 7). It included submissions from voluntary organisations such as the Church Army, the Salvation Army, and St. Mungo's which confirmed that the number of people in their shelters who have a recent history of mental disorder is rising. While there is evidence to suggest that long-stay patients are generally discharged only after extensive preparations have been made for their future accommodation (see for example *After Hospital: a study of long-term psychiatric patients in York* by Professor Kathleen Jones – ref. 8) the same may not be true for short-term patients, and people who have failed to gain admission to long-stay facilities with much tighter admissions criteria now in force. In London Kay and Legg in their report *Discharged to the Community* (ref. 9) have summarised the experience of former psychiatric patients as follows:

- Patients had little involvement, choice or control in the discharge decisions, or in arrangements for rehousing and for day care; most received no practical advice or information on welfare benefits or medication before discharge
- There was consistent evidence of better treatment for those selected by professionals as the 'deserving' mentally ill; these people experienced more preparation, discussion and choice and more later moved to specialist or supported accommodation
- Although the majority preferred living outside hospital, 80% were dissatisfied with their current housing; many living in temporary accommodation (emergency homeless accommodation or social services hostels) were critical of the rules, regimes and enforced community; others living in independent housing alone or with their families were particularly concerned about their physical housing conditions
- Despite a high level of contact with statutory services, nearly 40% said they wanted more support, particularly from social workers; over a quarter said that coping with their mental illness was their main problem; and over 40% experienced a range of problems in claiming welfare benefits
- In the future 75% wanted their own independent housing and to choose with whom they lived; nearly half wanted paid employment and over a third wanted more on-going support.

A significant group of men who had been residing for years at the DHSS's Camberwell Resettlement Unit (CRU) were deemed as being in need of long-stay hospital provision. Following assessment by consultants, the four RHAs for London agreed to admit about 40 patients. In addition, a survey in April 1985 of the remaining 45 residents at the CRU, prior to its closure, concluded that 15 were suffering from severe mental illnesses, ten individuals having been diagnosed as chronic schizophrenics.

Services for Elderly People

30. Services for elderly people face different problems. There are no large hospitals specifically for the elderly to compare with the old psychiatric hospitals. But there are many long-stay wards in hospitals that could be replaced by community-based services to advantage; and many people in residential homes who do not need to be there.

31. As the Commission's earlier report, *Managing Social Services for the*

Elderly More Effectively (ref. 10) made clear, a significant increase in the number of people aged over 85 (the so called 'elderly elderly' who need most support to remain in the community) is in prospect over the next decade. Investigations by the Commission's auditors in 1985 showed that few local authority social services departments have agreed plans in advance for meeting the increase in need and demand for community care that this demographic trend will inevitably bring with it. Meanwhile, a White Paper published in 1981 *Growing Older* (ref. 2) was not specific about the pattern of services that should emerge for the elderly and added little to the policies already outlined in *Care in Action*. Table 9 shows that while there has been a decrease in reliance on hospital beds this has been more than offset through the growth in numbers of private residential homes.

Table 9: BALANCE OF CARE FOR ELDERLY PEOPLE
England and Wales

	1974		1979		1984	
	Nos.	Nos. per 1000 75+	Nos.	Nos. per 1000 75+	Nos.	Nos. per 1000 75+
Geriatric Hospitals (occupied beds)	54,600	22.1	54,500	19.6	54,100	17.1
LA Homes (occupied places)	98,600	40.0	109,100	39.3	109,200	34.5
Nursing Homes (long-stay occ. beds)	11,900	4.8	13,800	5.0	24,100	7.6
Voluntary Homes (occupied places)	23,300	9.5	25,600	9.2	26,900	8.5
Private Homes (occupied places)	19,300	7.8	26,800	9.7	55,000	17.4
Day Patient (attendances/day)	4,100	1.7	5,000	1.8	7,000	2.2
LA Day Centre (places)	13,800	5.6	29,100	10.5	34,400	10.9
Home Help staff (wte's)*	45,200	18.3	49,600	17.9	56,700	17.9
Meals (000's per year)*	35,200	14.3	43,300	15.6	45,000	14.2

* Numbers of home help staff (whole-time equivalents) and meals serve all client groups but are predominantly for elderly people.

32. The table shows that, apart from local authority day care between 1974 and 1979, domiciliary services which allow people to remain in their own homes have been struggling to keep pace with demographic trends.

UNEVEN RESPONSE

33. The slow progess is not universal. Progress in some authorities has been notable. But, national statistics indicate that the variation between authorities is considerable. Some variation between areas is to be expected because of differences in need. For example, Gibbons, Jennings and Wing have shown (ref. 11) in a study of eight psychiatric case registers, that there is a correlation between incidence of mental illness and the characteristics of an area – including immigration patterns and socio-demographic indices of poverty, unemployment, social isolation and ethnic groups. However, these differences do not account for more than a part of the variation observed even between similar authorities. Since the situation differs between client groups, each is discussed separately below.

34. Spending by local authorities on services for *mentally handicapped adults* varies by a factor of six to one. The biggest variation occurs within London. In 1984–5 the highest and lowest local authorities in terms of gross expenditure per head of population are as follows (with £3 per head of population equivalent to about £1,500 for every mentally handicapped adult on average):

Inner London:	Camden £11.65, Wandsworth £5.51
Outer London:	Hillingdon £9.26, Sutton £2.04
Metropolitan Districts:	Coventry £8.16, North Tyneside £3.46
Counties:	Powys £6.56, Isle of Wight £3.25

Exhibit 3 shows the variation in expenditure levels between authorities.

Exhibit 3

LOCAL AUTHORITY GROSS EXPENDITURE ON SERVICES FOR MENTALLY HANDICAPPED PEOPLE
£ per Head of Population, England and Wales 1984-5

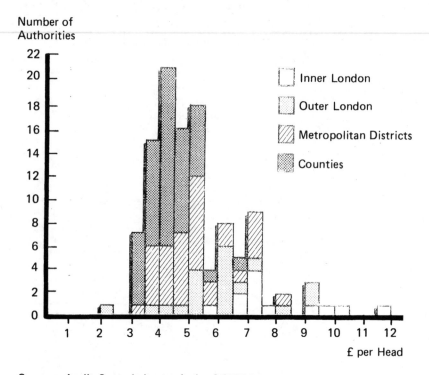

Source: Audit Commission analysis of CIPFA
Personal Social Services Statistics

35. By contrast, the expenditure on mentally handicapped in-patients across RHAs is relatively constant (£7.80 per head to £10.30 per head) with the exception of two regions which for historical reasons have a large number of mental handicap hospitals – South Western RHA (£14.00) and South West Thames RHA (£17.50). There is little evidence of any correlation between RHA and social services department spending on mentally handicapped people.

36. An even wider spread of expenditure can be observed for services for *mentally ill people*, as illustrated in Exhibit 4. Given the likelihood that over 5 million people will be consulting their general practitioner about a mental health problem every year with 600,000 being referred to specialist services, it will be evident that annual expenditure of less than £2 for every local resident (i.e. some £160 a year per client referred for specialist care, on average) is likely to provide a community service in name only – it would buy every client perhaps no more than one visit a month from a social worker. Fewer than one local authority in five meets this very limited standard at present.

37. Expenditure per resident is highest in Newcastle and Inner London. The incidence of mental illness is thought to be proportionately greatest in inner city areas. Newcastle spends £7.43 per head of population. Two Inner London boroughs (Wandsworth £6.68 and Westminster £6.36) spend over £6 per head of population and only one (Greenwich £2.05) spends less than £3. In Outer London the range is from £3.90 (Harrow) down to 49p

Exhibit 4

**LOCAL AUTHORITY GROSS EXPENDITURE ON
SERVICES FOR MENTALLY ILL PEOPLE**

£ per Head of Population, England and Wales 1984-5

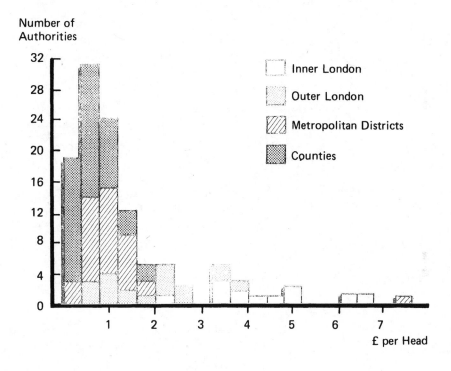

Source: Audit Commission analysis of CIPFA
Personal Social Services Statistics

(Redbridge). Gwynedd (£1.77) is the highest spending county. The highest spending Metropolitan district after Newcastle (£7.43) is Oldham (£1.69). Four counties (Cornwall, Gloucestershire, Northumberland and Oxfordshire) spend less than 20 pence per head of population on mentally ill people.

38. There is also a wide variation in in-patient provision for mentally ill people at the RHA level. The number of resident patients per 1000 population varies from 0.8 in Oxford RHA to 2.0 in Mersey RHA. The expenditure on mental illness in-patients per head of total population varies from £11.40 in Oxford RHA to £25.00 in Mersey RHA (i.e. £14,700 a year per resident patient in Oxford RHA and £12,200 in Mersey). In spite of wide variations in local authority and health authority spending on mentally ill people, there is no correlation between the two at the regional level. This may in part be due to regional transfers, with the cluster of hospitals at Epsom in particular serving several regions.

39. Similarly local authority expenditure on *elderly people* (gross expenditure on residential day and domiciliary services, per person over 75) varies by a factor of five to one as shown in Exhibit 5. The highest and lowest spenders by authority type are as follows:

Inner London:	Islington £1,009, Wandsworth £637
Outer London:	Haringey £699, Sutton £294
Metropolitan Districts:	Manchester £613, Sefton £290
Counties:	Cleveland £481, West Sussex £184

40. As the Commission pointed out in its report *Managing Social Services for the Elderly More Effectively* (ref. 10) 15% of the elderly population accounts for virtually all the annual expenditure of over £1.5 billion spent on direct services for elderly people provided by local authority social services departments. Therefore, at the local level, expenditure is likely to vary depending on:

(a) The proportion of elderly people in residential care: the provision of local authority residential accommodation for the elderly ranges from under 20 places for every 1,000 people aged over 75 to over 60 places

(b) The balance of local authority social services provisions for elderly people: at one extreme, less than 40% of LA expenditure is on residential care; at the other end of the spectrum, is nearly 80% devoted to residential care

(c) The level of provision of private and voluntary residential accommodation for the elderly: this varies from 7.6 for every 1,000 people aged 75 and over in Cleveland to ten times that amount in Devon. It would be reasonable to expect to see some relationship between levels of private and voluntary residential care provision on the one hand and local authority social services provision on the other

(d) The unit cost of the residential accommodation. A recent study (ref. 12) for the DHSS by Ernst & Whinney showed a very wide variation in the costs per resident week of private and voluntary residential homes for the elderly; CIPFA statistics reveal a less marked, but nonetheless substantial, variation in unit costs within the local government sector as Table 10 indicates.

Exhibit 5

LOCAL AUTHORITY GROSS EXPENDITURE ON SERVICES FOR ELDERLY PEOPLE

£ per Person over 75, England and Wales 1984-5

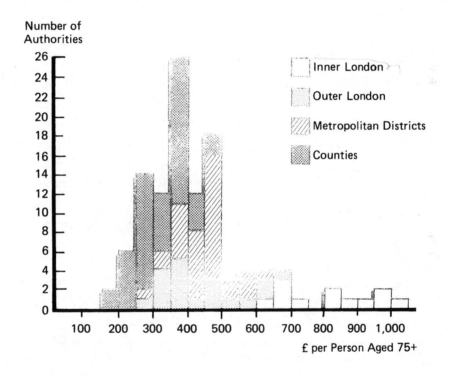

Source: Audit Commission analysis of CIPFA
        Personal Social Services Statistics

Table 10: COSTS OF RESIDENTIAL HOMES FOR THE ELDERLY, 1985
£ per resident week

	Lowest	Mean	Highest
Local Authority Homes*	£85.9 per week	110.9	185.1
Private Homes	36.3	117.3	247.2
Voluntary Homes	21.2	90.2	202.1

* Figures for local authority homes are based on the average costs of all homes within an authority. The statistics do not provide costs for individual homes.

41. Some indications of the unevenness of the response to the community care initiative is provided by analysis of local differences in expenditure on home helps, as shown in Exhibit 6. The home help service, wardens of sheltered accommodation, general medical practitioners and community nurses are the keys to community care for the elderly. Yet home help provision varies by a factor of six or more among authorities – from under seven full-time home helps for every 1,000 people aged over 75 (equivalent to less than eight minutes of active help every week for each person aged over 75) to 44 full-time home helps. And the relative importance of the home help service in terms of social services expenditure varies widely as well, from 13% of social service department expenditure on the elderly to nearly 40%.

Exhibit 6

HOME HELP NUMBERS AND EXPENDITURE

England and Wales 1984-5

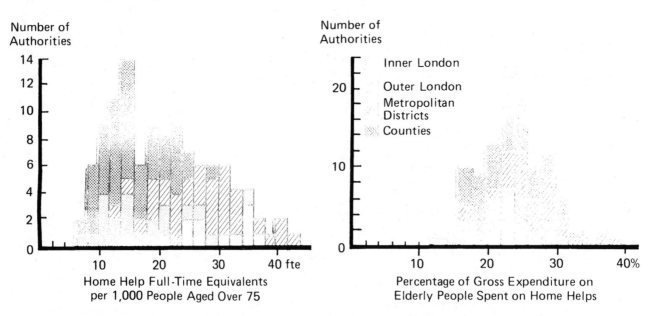

Source: Audit Commission analysis of CIPFA
Personal Social Services Statistics

42. Again by contrast, NHS geriatric in-patient expenditure does not vary so much at the regional level. The range of costs, per person over 75, is from £220 (South Western RHA) to £340 (Mersey RHA). Furthermore, no relationship can be found between RHA spending on geriatric in-patients and social service departments' expenditure on services for the elderly.

43. In addition to the unevenness of social services expenditure, social security spending on care is also uneven, in two ways. First, the rules for benefits make it easier to obtain private residential care rather than private domiciliary care – in direct contrast to community care policies. Second, the take-up of Supplementary Benefits payments for board and lodging

(independent homes) is not evenly distributed across the country. Exhibit 7 shows the uneven distribution of residential homes.

Exhibit 7

ELDERLY RESIDENTS IN PRIVATE AND VOLUNTARY HOMES, 31 MARCH, 1985

Residents per 1,000 people aged 75+

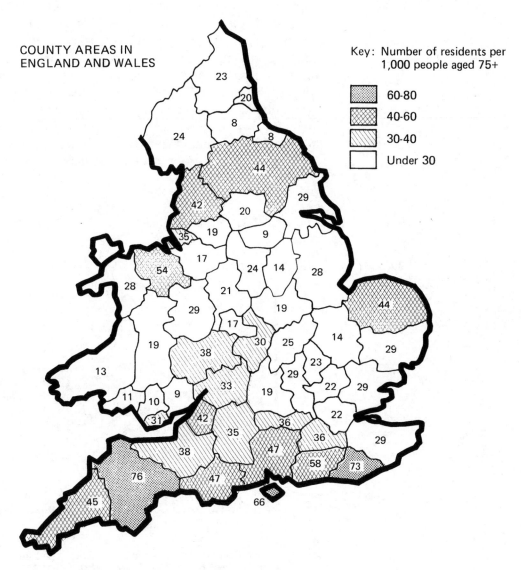

Source: DHSS RA3 returns for 31 March, 1985

The number of supplementary benefit claimants broadly follows the same regional distribution (see Table D-4 in Appendix D). The highest concentrations of private and voluntary homes are in the seaside resorts – Devon, East Sussex, the Isle of Wight and Sefton. These areas are where many elderly people choose to live and higher provision is therefore appropriate. But the Exhibit shows **the provision per thousand people aged over 75** and it is evident that people in the seaside areas have greater relative access to facilities than people living elsewhere.

44. Although the four seaside authorities above have some of the lowest provision rates for local authority residential accommodation for the elderly, they are nevertheless the top four authorities in terms of total private and public provisions per person over 75. Analysis shows that local authorities where there are most private and voluntary places for the elderly have the

following characteristics:

  – Lower than average need for such care for each elderly person, as measured by the Rate Support Grant (RSG) indicator E14 for social services for the elderly
  – Lower than average social service department spending on the elderly, per person over 75
  – Lower than average sheltered housing units, per person over 75.

However, apart from these authorities there is little overall relationship between the levels of local authority and private sector provision of residential accommodation for the elderly, as Exhibit 8 shows. As a result, the growth of the private and voluntary sector has had the simultaneous perverse effects of attracting Supplementary Benefits support for people receiving residential rather than community care who live in areas of the country where the need for care per person over 75 is, if anything, below average. Any adjustment would be difficult, however, because it would involve a change to the rules for Supplementary Benefits. This would in turn mean a fundamental change to individuals' entitlement to benefits, rather than an adjustment to a formula for distributing funds.

Exhibit 8

TOTAL RESIDENTIAL CARE FOR THE ELDERLY, MARCH 1985

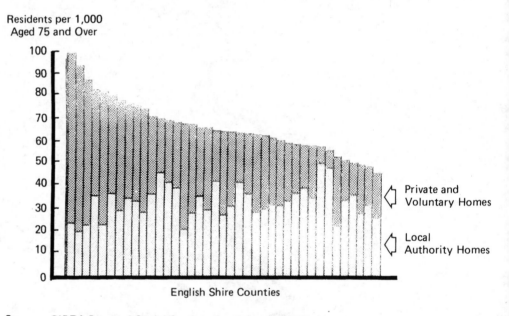

Residents per 1,000 Aged 75 and Over

English Shire Counties

Private and Voluntary Homes

Local Authority Homes

Source: CIPFA Personal Social Services Statistics, 1984-85 Actuals
DHSS tabulation of RA3 returns for March 1985

UNATTRACTIVE PROSPECTS

45. If nothing changes, the outlook is bleak. Community care policies are being adopted to a limited degree only, with slow and uneven progress across the country. For mentally ill and elderly people the following trends are evident:

  (a) Long-stay hospital provision is being reduced at a significant rate, on a pro-rata basis for elderly people and absolutely for the mentally ill
  (b) But local authority community-based services are not expanding sufficiently rapidly to offset the rundown in NHS accommodation; and no one knows what has happened to many of the patients that have been discharged
  (c) Provision of community-based local authority support services is very uneven; in some areas it is close to non-existent for mentally ill people in particular

(d) Numbers of residential homes and hence the number of residents who claim Supplementary Benefit payments for board and lodging – particularly elderly people – are expanding, often without supporting services such as day centres. Furthermore, provision of private residential homes is growing unevenly, with high numbers per head of population aged over 75 on the South Coast.

At best, there has been a shift in services from old remote long-stay hospitals to new long-stay residential homes, missing out a wider range of more flexible, more cost-effective forms of community care on the way. At worst, and particularly for the mentally ill, there is an inadequate service. Even for mentally handicapped people, progress is slow. Of course, some development of community services can be expected over the next few years – but at such a slow pace that the goal of a primarily community-based service supporting people in their own homes will remain as distant as ever.

46. In short, the community care initiative will largely have failed. Instead, a new framework based on residential homes will have replaced hospital beds. While this will almost certainly provide an improvement in some areas, it will be unnecessarily expensive; it will be inappropriate for many people; and it will not provide the range of options for improving the quality of life. Furthermore, the uneven provision will either mean that many people will be accommodated miles from their relatives and community; or if available services are largely used by local people, the standards of service will vary markedly from area to area. In any event, opportunities for improvements in services and value for money will have been lost, since community care can be less expensive than residential care for individual people as Table 11 indicates for the two examples discussed earlier (in paragraph 13).

Table 11: TYPICAL COSTS
        £ per week 1986 prices

	ILLUSTRATIVE	
Care Setting	Example A	Example B
Community Care	£ 97.35 per week	132.50
Residential Care		
– local authority	133.25	190.25
– private and voluntary	138.55	209.55
NHS Hospitals	294.75	254.75

47. In particular, poor value for money results for the taxpayer because less effective and efficient forms of care persist; much of the replacement for hospitals is in the form of residential and nursing home care; and more effective community services are not being adequately developed. Moreover other people may require more care which is currently not available, so that there is a mis-match between services and people.

*   *   *

48. The run-down of old long-stay hospitals and the increase in numbers of elderly people both require major initiatives in service development over the next 15 years. But the opportunity for building a community-based service will not remain open indefinitely: once an alternative service based on residential homes is in place, vested interests and institutional inertia can be expected to block any major changes in patterns of care. However, before considering what corrective action needs to be taken, the underlying causes of the present position must be understood. The Commission's analysis of these causes is set out in the next chapter.

2. Fundamental Underlying Problems

49. There are a number of factors causing difficulties with the introduction of community care. Some result from the greater complexity of organising care in the community and from the difficulties of managing change. These are unavoidable and are an inherent aspect of the implementation process. However, there are also difficulties which should be avoidable.

50. One reason that is frequently advanced to explain the slow progress is a lack of finance. However, a much wider range of community based services could be provided within present levels of funding – although, as with all health and personal social services, more money can always be put to good use. Increased funding is, at best, only part of the answer to the problems described in the previous chapter. At worst, it could mask, temporarily at least, the need for some basic changes in the way that care for mentally ill, mentally handicapped, physically handicapped and elderly people is provided and paid for. The Commission has concluded that the slow and uneven progress towards community care is due to some fundamental underlying problems which need to be tackled directly:

(i) Although out of the total amounts of money being spent (some £6 billion a year) there should be enough to provide at least a much improved level of community-based services, the methods for distributing the available finance do not match the requirements of community care policies.

(ii) Additional short-term bridging finance is required to fund the transition to community care.

(iii) Social security policies are undermining any switch from residential to community care.

(iv) A fragmented organisation structure causes delays and difficulties; and there has been a failure to adapt systems and structures to accommodate the shift in policy.

(v) Staffing arrangements are inadequate, with a failure to provide sufficient re-training for existing staff in hospitals and to recruit the additional staff required in the community.

These underlying causes of the problems with community care are considered in turn in the rest of this chapter.

MISMATCH RESOURCES

51. The House of Commons Select Committee maintained (ref. 7) that 'the proposition that community care could be cost-neutral is untenable' and recommended 'that the Government now accept that genuine community care policies are achievable only in the context of some real increase over a period of years in expenditure on services for mentally handicapped and mentally ill people'. However, as Table 12 shows, total expenditure in 1984–5 actually exceeds the earliest White Paper targets when these are expressed in 1984–5 unit costs and prices.

Table 12: COMPARISON OF THE COST OF THE WHITE PAPER TARGET VERSUS ACTUAL PROVISION
England only, 1984–5

			Total Cost £m	
	Actual Provision	White Paper Target	Actual	White Paper Target
Mentally Handicapped Adults				
Hospital In-patient Beds	40,300	25,800	461	295
Day Patient Places	1,300	4,700	5	19
Hospital Out-patients	–	–	1	1
NHS Administration and Other	–	–	31	21
Residential Care	17,400	28,200	98	160
Day Care ATCs	47,500	70,500	107	158
Social Workers	–	–	23	36
LA Other, Administration and Training	–	–	45	70
Total cost			771	760
Mentally Ill Adults				
Hospital In-patient Beds	78,900	47,900	901	547
Day Patient Places	17,000	45,800	60	163
Hospital Out-Patients	–	–	62	62
NHS Administration and Other	–	–	68	51
Residential Care	6,800	11,500	21	35
Day Care	9,000	28,200	18	56
Social Workers	–	–	4	10
LA Other, Administration and Training	–	–	9	21
Total Cost			1,143	945

52. The public funds for community care are largely determined by three separate sources; the DOE and the two sides of DHSS (health and social security). The DOE co-ordinates local government policies and finance; the DHSS (health/social services) co-ordinates health service and social services policies; and the DHSS (social security) co-ordinates income support and maintenance. Personal social services are thus in a position where a substantial part of the finance falls primarily in the field of one central government department (DOE) whilst other finance and central government policy are the responsibility of another (DHSS). The sums involved have already been described but can be roughly summarised as £2 billion for local social services (DOE), £3 billion via the health service (DHSS) and £1 billion via social security to purchase or support 'care' as opposed to accommodation or income maintenance (DHSS).

53. There is no single answer to the question: how much should community care cost? There are a number of different variables which must be taken into account in addition to finance including: quality of life, risk, choice, level of dependency and model of care chosen:

– The quality of life of people can be improved by providing additional cover by support staff, day care facilities, better accommodation etc
– Some community care options may carry different degrees of risk to the person in the community. A service with night cover involves lower risks (and higher costs) than a service without such cover. Some options may involve high risk but equivalent higher quality of life than others (own independent home with support rather than communal living in a hostel – although some people may prefer communal living)

- Offering an element of choice may cost more, since more alternatives must be provided in sufficient quantity to provide the choice.

All of these factors affect clients and their families differently; there are no universal prescriptions for the 'right' mode of care for a person of a given level of dependency. The Government's response to the Select Committee pointed out that 'for some individuals community care will be cheaper than existing provision. For others – particularly where the baseline of existing institutional facilities is inadequate – it will be more expensive'.

54. Also, the model of care adopted affects costs. Services based heavily on the medical model – with higher levels of in-patient care – are likely to be much more expensive. Services based on more radical alternatives – such as those described in chapter 3 – are likely to be less expensive. But direct comparison would need to take account of the variables listed above.

55. The view taken by managers who have successfully built community-based services locally is that the question should be viewed the other way around: what can be done with the money available? It is always easy to spend more money and always easy to blame a lack of money for a lack of activity. The two case examples of Plymouth and Torquay already mentioned and described more fully in chapter 3 demonstrate that an acceptable community care service *can* be provided to meet current needs at no extra cost in revenue terms to health and social services (although with additional cost to the social security system, which is not cash limited). Of course, funding services for the elderly must allow for demographic trends.

56. The adequacy of the total level of funding of services for different client groups is not discussed further in this report, partly because it involves complex value judgements as outlined above; and partly because it involves political judgements beyond the remit of the Commission. Instead, having established that it is possible to provide a community care service within existing funding levels, the report considers what can be done to make the best of what resources exist. The first requirement is that the pattern of distribution of funds must match policy objectives and requirements. The Government's policies for community care involve a change from care in residential settings to care in people's own homes in the community; they also require a corresponding shift from health service provision to social services provision, as well as changes in the nature of the provision made by both types of authority. However the way funds are distributed does not adequately allow for this shift. Furthermore, it does not match the requirements of the Government's own community care policies, causing policy conflicts.

57. There are three basic problems that need to be addressed, which are discussed further below:

(i) The way in which NHS resources are determined and allocated to regions does not make any provision for the shift of services and responsibility for funding them from the NHS to local authority social services departments.

(ii) The present systems for distributing Rate Support Grant (RSG) act as a deterrent to the expansion of community-based services in many local authorities.

(iii) The arrangements for joint NHS/local authority financing of community services are inadequate in scale, and face serious practical problems in operation. Local authorities are in the position of having to invest – often attracting Ministerial criticism for increasing staffing levels in the process – in order to enable the NHS to save money.

58. NHS finance is determined and distributed separately from local authority finance. At the centre it is almost impossible under present arrangements to adjust the total health service budget to take account of the extent to which responsibility has been transferred to local authorities. Similarly the way the money is distributed to the regions takes no account of the transfer of responsibility. RHAs receive their allocation of funds through the RAWP formula (determined by the Resource Allocation Working Party in 1976 ref. 13). For revenue funds this is based on analyses of NHS expenditure for six service categories:

- Non-psychiatric in-patients services
- Day patients and out-patients services
- Community services
- Ambulance services
- Mental illness hospital in-patient services
- Mental handicap hospital in-patient services.

For each service, a weighted population of each region is calculated to take account of demographic factors such as age, sex and 'standardised mortality ratios' (which link a relatively high death rate to relatively high demand for non-psychiatric services). The six weighted populations are combined in proportion to previous years' expenditure on the six services. This combined weighted population, with adjustment to take account of the London weighting on pay scales and an increment for the service costs associated with medical teaching establishes each region's target share of the available resources. Each year, Ministers decide, in the light of factors such as the increase in total resources available for health authority spending, what pace of change towards regional targets would be appropriate. The RAWP formula itself does not mathematically determine regions' financial allocations for any particular year.

59. The RAWP formula is designed as a tool to equalise the allocation of aggregate funds at the regional level. It is not intended to influence authorities' relative spending on different services, nor to reflect DHSS priorities. In fact, because it is based on past expenditure it lags rather than leads any shift in services. The main effect of the formula over the last ten years has been to shift the balance away from the four Thames regions (they were up to 17% above target) in favour of other regions (e.g. North Western and Trent that were 12% below target). The transfer has been undertaken gradually so that for 1986–7 all regions are in the range 96 – 108% of target (compared to 91–113% in 1979–80).

60. However, while the RAWP formula adjusts between relative health needs it does not make any provision for the shift of services and responsibility for funding them from health to local authorities. It has a community care component; but this is health service community care (community nurses etc). A region in which many people have been discharged into the community to be looked after by social services is treated in exactly the same way in the formula as a region with fewer people transferred. The distribution of funds below regional level is more flexible, although many RHAs apply a modified version of the RAWP formula. The Health Service Planning System allows some adjustment to take account of developments locally; but regions cannot be expected to be aware of local authority activities since they are not part of the planning system.

Deterrent Effect of Rate Support Grant on Local Authorities

61. Local authorities receive their funds from Rate Support Grant (RSG) and locally levied rates and charges for services. The amount of money raised through rates is a matter for local discretion, subject to guidelines and constraints set by central government. The amount of grant received depends on:

(a) The Aggregate Exchequer Grant which is the total amount of money available to support local government spending. It reflects the Government's desire to restrain local government expenditure in total, and not its enthusiasm for spending on individual services. The Government's expenditure plans for future local government spending are published each year in the Public Expenditure White Paper, although these plans cannot be imposed directly on local authorities

(b) The distribution of grant between authorities, which is based on the Grant Related Expenditure (GRE) formula that measures 'need' and on local 'resources'. This distribution is designed to split total grants between authorities, and not between services

(c) The level of spending of authorities – since any increase in spending will, for most authorities, result in a reduced level of grant. The effect is more severe for authorities spending well above GRE. Ultimately 'rate capping' can be used by the Government to prevent local authorities increasing rates to make up for grant lost in this way, with 16 authorities responsible for personal social services due to be rate-capped in 1987–8.

62. In recent years, the Government has been restraining local authority spending in total in accordance with its public expenditure policies. At the same time community care policies are being endorsed that require an expansion of social services spending. Because community care policies require a *shift* in expenditure from health rather than any increase in public sector expenditure there should be no conflict of interest. In practice, such a shift would require complex adjustments. Thus, in order to promote social services expenditure, the Government would have to build in a higher priority for social services by raising personal social services GRE control totals by a higher proportion than for other services (in which case authorities with personal social services would tend to receive more grant); or by introducing specific grants (there being none for personal social services at present). However, to date, neither mechanism has been used and no additional provision has been made for local authority community care services. In fact, attempts by many local authorities to increase expenditure to fund community care on their own initiative have been heavily penalised by loss of grant.

63. It is true that over past years an increase of 2% has usually been included in the Government's expenditure plans to reflect demographic and similar pressures to which personal social services are subject. But the only component directly relevant to community care policies was 0.7% for the take-up of the joint finance taper. However, the Secretary of State for Social Services announced at the Social Services Annual Conference on 19 September 1986 that:

'Looking to the future, the provisional rate support grant settlement for 1987–8 announced in July shows a very substantial increase in total provision for local authorities. . . The provisional allocation for personal social services allows for a full $3\frac{1}{2}$% increase on top of provision for inflation. Of this $2\frac{1}{2}$% will fully meet demographic and other pressures which these services face. That leaves *for the first time* (emphasis added) a figure of 1% – or £27 million – to enable authorities to build up their community care service'.

But other changes made in the overall arrangements for 1987–8 will detract from this addition. For example, GRE totals which help determine the grant actually received by local authorities will be increased by about 5% less than allowed for in the settlement. Furthermore, even if GRE totals are adjusted to take account of community care policies any resultant increase in grant could be applied by local decision to other heads of expenditure. Central government may exhort local government to shift funds into social services, and social services to shift funds into community care, but local government is perfectly at liberty to follow some other course of action if it so wishes, and if an authority is facing severe cutbacks or high rate increases, some sharing of cuts across budget heads is usual. Hence the amount filtering through does not necessarily match Government expenditure plans.

64. Virtually all authorities that provide social services lose grant if they increase spending in real terms. So apart from the proposed provisional increase, in the current climate of restraints on local government expenditure, those authorities that wish to develop community care policies must either make equivalent cuts elsewhere in their budgets, or they must transfer a disproportionately high burden of cost onto local ratepayers as Table 13 shows:

Table 13: ACTUAL COST TO LOCAL RATEPAYERS OF AN ADDITIONAL £1 MILLION OF EXPENDITURE ON COMMUNITY CARE
Examples: Illustrative sample of authorities

Wakefield	£1.16 million
Cornwall	1.30
Norfolk	1.57
Cleveland	1.74
Sheffield	1.75
Sandwell	1.81
Lambeth	2.00
Croydon	2.00

Hence, the system used to control expenditure can penalise local ratepayers in authorities implementing government policy and saving money for the NHS into the bargain. Thus in one authority visited that had pioneered community care for mentally handicapped people in accordance with the Government's guidelines, heavy grant losses were being incurred because the authority was exceeding its GRE in part as a result of this policy. The service implications of community care policies are demonstrated by the large proportion of the staffing changes in local authorities over the last three years attributable to social services departments. Table 14 provides the details:

Table 14: LOCAL AUTHORITY STAFF CHANGES – 1983 TO 1986
England only. Whole-Time Equivalents

	March 1983 actual	March 1986 provisional	Change no.	%
Social Services	202,400	217,300	14,900	7.4%
Miscellaneous Services	232,300	237,800	5,500	2.4
Housing	52,000	57,300	5,300	10.3
Recreation, Parks and Baths	69,500	72,400	3,000	4.3
Public Libraries and Museums	31,200	32,200	1,000	3.1
Fire Service	38,700	39,300	600	1.5
Town and Country Planning	19,700	19,900	200	1.2
Environmental Health	19,800	19,200	(500)	(2.6)
Transport	18,000	17,100	(1,000)	(5.3)
Refuse Collection and Disposal	41,400	37,400	(4,000)	(9.7)
Construction	108,400	104,200	(4,200)	(3.9)
Education	881,000	870,600	(10,500)	(1.2)
All General Services	1,714,300	1,724,600	10,300	0.6

Note: Figures in parentheses are reductions in staffing levels.

65. The Commission has already published detailed reports on the shortcomings of the present arrangements for distributing block grant and controlling capital spending (ref. 17) within local authorities. These general shortcomings adversely affect the community care programme in many areas. In particular the elderly are the only 'community care' group specifically identified in the RSG formulae; and the numbers of mentally handicapped, mentally ill and younger physically handicapped people supported by local authorities are not taken into account at all. No way has been found to take into account at the local level other inputs such as the provision of service by district health authorities or the support for residents of private and voluntary homes (which can vary significantly between authorities – see Exhibit 8). More specifically it does not make any allowance for the extent to which community care policies are being introduced.

Inadequate Joint Finance and Financial Transfers

66. The Government has recognised that the existing structure of local government finance is ill-suited to the direct encouragement of policies for community care, and as a result has introduced more direct measures. These involve either the direct transfer of funds by health authorities themselves to local authorities, or joint financing.

67. *Joint Finance* was originally a source of funds provided to health authorities to be spent by mutual agreement on social services' projects of benefit to the NHS. The amount of joint finance expenditure increased rapidly from its introduction in 1976 until 1980, but it has increased only modestly in real terms since then (as Table 15 shows). During the late 1970s expenditure was divided equally between capital and revenue. Now, with local authorities becoming increasingly concerned about the long-term revenue implications of capital schemes, the use of Joint Finance is dominated by revenue spending.

Table 15: JOINT FINANCE EXPENDITURE
£ million, at 1984–5 prices

Year	Capital	Revenue	Total	% Revenue of Total
1976–7	£ 6.6m	2.7	9.3	29%
1977–8	18.1	17.4	35.5	49
1978–9	29.0	29.2	58.2	50
1979–80	26.0	37.1	63.1	59
1980–1	30.6	48.7	79.3	61
1981–2	27.7	57.8	85.5	68
1982–3	28.9	62.1	91.0	68
1983–4	22.2	68.9	91.1	76
1984–5	22.4	74.2	96.6	77

68. Joint finance is intended to provide 'pump priming' funds only; the funding of schemes must be transferred in due course from joint finance to the agency judged to be most directly responsible. Local authorities are becoming increasingly reluctant to accept the long-term commitments that such funding implies, even though in the past commitments picked up from joint finance were excluded from penalties (i.e. 'disregarded') and thus provided a way for authorities to expand their base budgets without incurring significant loss of grant. With the recent change in the system and abolition of penalties (and consequently disregards) this situation no longer applies; and any extension in base budget to pick up joint finance commitments not covered by the increase in the GRE totals leads to reduced grant in the normal way. As a result a significant proportion is now being spent either on health authority schemes (18% of total joint finance expenditure in 1984–5) or the voluntary bodies (7%). The limited duration of joint finance schemes precludes the use of this form of finance as a permanent way of effecting the

shift from the NHS to personal social services. The Select Committee concluded that 'joint finance is still an essential part of the infrastructure of community care; but as a means of transferring further responsibilities from the NHS to local authorities it is now virtually played out'. [However as a way of bridging the costs of starting new services, joint finance is still very useful as described below.]

69. *Direct transfer of funds* is a more recent, and longer-term mechanism introduced through a circular (ref.14) in 1983 following the consultative document *Care in the Community* published in 1981 (ref.15). This mechanism (known as 'the dowry') allows the transfer of health authority funds direct to social services departments, usually as responsibility for patients is transferred.

70. However, useful as this mechanism is initially, it is limited in scope – total expenditure directly transferred is estimated by the Commission to be no more than £10–20 million a year; and it is flawed in a number of ways:

- The transfer of funds is usually linked to patients discharged from psychiatric or mental handicap hospitals only. Local authorities meanwhile are faced not only by people who would always have come their way, but also by people discharged from long-stay care *and* people no longer admitted to long-stay care in the first place. One or two authorities are transferring services wholesale, together with the associated finance. But otherwise no transfer takes place to fund people in the community requiring services who have not managed to gain admission to either type of hospital

- At a time of restraint in local government finance, funding of the build-up of community services is dependent upon the run-down of hospitals. However, transfer payments are usually only made *after* a transfer has taken place, and often only to approved services. In such circumstances, community care needs to be in place before the run-down of hospitals. This causes a cashflow problem for the local authority which incurs the cost before receiving the 'dowry'

- Many residents of long-stay hospitals will not be discharged into the community, and will live out their lives in hospital. In this event no finance is transferred at all – even though there are others in the community requiring services (although some regions set aside such money for use for the patient group concerned)

- Where people are placed by health authorities directly into the private or voluntary sector (funded by Supplementary Benefits) no money is transferred – although day care services may be required

- In some regions the amount transferred to social services is less than the average hospital cost on the grounds that social security payments make up the difference.

These situations can lead to either an immediate or longer term switch of funds within health authorities away from the priority groups of elderly, mentally handicapped, mentally ill and physically handicapped people to other health services. This 'leakage' reduces the overall funds available for community care.

71. To overcome these problems, several local authorities are taking over the entire mental handicap service ('going for broke', as one director put it) in order to secure adequate finances for the service in the future. Apart from this approach, which obviously requires the collaboration of the local health authority, there is no mechanism to ensure that the funds transferred in any way match the responsibilities transferred. Direct transfer of funds relies on the benevolence and altruism of health authorities. Such sentiments tend to be in short supply in times of economic restraint. As it was put to the team by one district general manager, on no account was he going to transfer funds

while acute services in his district were in his view under-funded – especially as he was faced with the problem of finding additional savings to finance part of pay awards within the health service. Another district general manager observed that 'local authorities are very good at joint planning the use of our money'.

72. Moreover, the present transfer mechanism provides a perverse incentive for local authorities to delay building up community-based services. Costs to ratepayers change as additional people are supported by the local authority under different circumstances. The 'true cost' is the actual cost of the extra services. However, in an authority facing 'negative grant' on additional expenditure, the cost to the ratepayers may exceed the true cost because the cost also includes the grant lost. Alternatively, in a local authority that has worked out a deal with the health authority to fund all additional costs (for example Plymouth described more fully in chapter 3) the cost to ratepayers may be zero. Finally, where a local authority is able to negotiate the maximum transfer payment from the health authority and simultaneously maximises the income from Supplementary Benefits, the local authority may actually make a 'profit' on the transfer which is further enhanced by an increase in government grant. Exhibit 9 illustrates the scale of the cost per client for the local ratepayers under different approaches to funding the transfer of a mentally handicapped adult from hospital (annual cost £13,000) to a group home (annual cost with day and domiciliary services of £3,500) depending on the local authorities' grant and spending position.

Exhibit 9

CHANGING COST TO RATEPAYERS OF DIFFERENT STRATEGIES

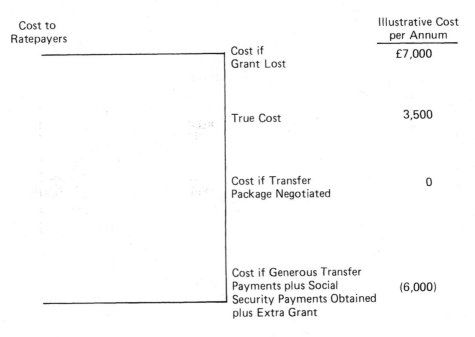

Cost to Ratepayers		Illustrative Cost per Annum
	Cost if Grant Lost	£7,000
	True Cost	3,500
	Cost if Transfer Package Negotiated	0
	Cost if Generous Transfer Payments plus Social Security Payments Obtained plus Extra Grant	(6,000)

Source: Audit Commission Example

Hence the current arrangement penalises the progressive authority and rewards the laggards who are reluctant to initiate community care schemes. This situation is clearly unsatisfactory.

73. Indeed, one effect of the introduction of transfer payments may actually have been to slow down the implementation of community care: some authorities that were previously pressing ahead with the introduction of new schemes at their own expense, are now no longer prepared to fund such

developments and are instead pressing health authorities to transfer the necessary finance. If the health authorities are not willing or able to make transfer funds available, everything stops.

74. Even after transfer funding has been agreed, the status of the transferred funds is often unclear:

- Are they eventually to be a contribution to local authorities' base budget, in which case they may result in a reduced level of grant
- Are they a payment for services rendered, in which case does the health authority retain some residual responsibility, e.g. to meet subsequent increases in costs
- Who controls them? The money transferred comes from the health authority but has usually (but not always) been transferred in perpetuity to the local authority.

Concern was expressed to the study team that NHS funds could be transferred by the local authority to other budget heads, with health service money being used to mend the roads, for example; or the transfer could be used to reduce overall expenditure. Consequently there are signed contracts ('memoranda of agreement') underpinning the transfer.

75. In short, it is evident that while the current arrangements for joint finance and transferring funds to local authorities have helped in some situations, some more appropriate mechanism for redistributing funds at source is required. Indeed the consultative document referred to earlier hints that some more permanent arrangement will be required in due course.

LACK OF BRIDGING FINANCE

76. The mismatch between finance and service requirements is further exacerbated by a shortage of funding to bridge the transition to a community-based service. As the old hospitals run down, community services must be built up in parallel if the overall level of service is to be maintained. While the final cost of the community based service may be no more than the cost of the hospital based service, additional transition costs will be incurred during the period when both services are running in parallel. These transition costs occur because, as *Better Services for the Mentally Ill* recognises, savings and expenditure are not always simultaneous, for two reasons:

(a) There are set-up costs – both capital and revenue costs – of the new community services. Services have to be in place, prospective clients assessed and staff trained before clients or patients can start to receive the service. Capital is required – either for new buildings (where purpose-built facilities are required) or to purchase additional properties on the open market where appropriate

(b) Hospitals that are being run-down have overheads and it is not possible to reduce costs in line with bed numbers. Unit costs (cost per patient) inevitably rise during the run-down.

Revenue and capital costs need to be considered separately.

Revenue Costs

77. While it is difficult to calculate the set-up costs (because they are often 'buried' in a number of community services) it is relatively easy to calculate the additional run-down costs because costs and patient numbers in hospitals are accurately recorded. Exhibit 10 shows the situation at the national level for mental illness and mental handicap hospitals. The Exhibit shows that since 1976–7 the number of in-patient days has fallen by 21% for mental handicap hospitals and 20% for mental illness hospitals. However, expenditure has actually increased by 8% and 7% respectively in real terms (£95 million in total, excluding headquarters administration). As a result, unit costs have risen by a third. The major causes of these increased unit costs are the high fixed costs of these institutions, and the increase in numbers of staff

Exhibit 10

NHS IN-PATIENT COSTS FOR ENGLAND, 1977-85

Constant prices; Index: 1977 = 100

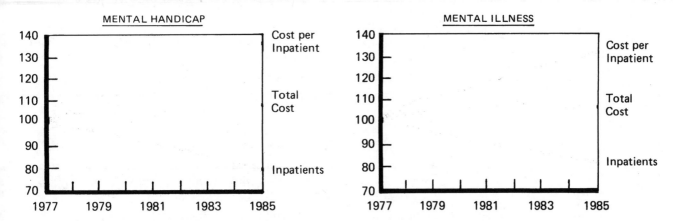

Source: Fourth Report from the Social Services Committee, 1985-86 Session
DHSS Statistical Bulletin 2/86

reflecting inadequate staffing levels in the past. The principal result of the community care initiative for many patients has thus been to improve the quality of care for those remaining in hospital – at a time when the policy is supposedly favouring care in the community.

78. The scale of the problem of bridging finance is large. In 1984–5 on average there were 10,200 fewer patients in mental handicap hospitals, and 16,800 fewer patients in mental illness hospitals than in 1976–7. Local authorities are having to meet the cost of services to replace these reductions; and the NHS must cover the extra £95 million for hospitals. It is these costs that must be bridged while the two services run in parallel.

79. As shown in Table 16 below, the actual real increase in total NHS and local authority expenditure over this period was £142 million for services for mentally handicapped people and £126 million for mentally ill people.

Table 16: NHS AND LOCAL AUTHORITY EXPENDITURE ON MENTAL HEALTH
England only. £ million at 1984–5 prices

	1976–7	1984–5	Increase
Mentally Handicapped Adults			
In-patient Costs	£427m	461	34
Out-patients and Day Patients	4	6	2
NHS Administration and Other	34	31	(3)
LA Residential Care	47	98	51
Adult Training Centres	76	106	30
Social Work and Other LA Costs	41	69	28
Total	629	771	142
Mentally Ill People			
In-patient Costs	840	901	61
Out-patients and Day Patients	75	122	47
NHS Administration and Other	71	68	(3)
LA Residential Care	14	21	7
LA Day Care	9	18	9
Social Work and Other LA Costs	8	13	5
Total	1,017	1,143	126

If it is assumed that the average unit costs of services for people placed in the community are the same as those for hospital patients, and that overall numbers remain roughly constant over time, it will be evident that the bridging finance is inadequate

- Total local authority expenditure on services for mentally handicapped people increased by little more than was necessary to cope with the needs of patients who would formerly have been admitted to hospital – budgeted expenditure on residential care, adult training centres and other local authority services in 1984–5 was £109 million higher in real terms than in 1976–7; but the cost of providing community-based care for the survivors of the 10,200 former patients and people 'following on' who have remained in the community instead of being admitted to hospital is likely to have been of the order of £130 million at NHS unit costs. While the cost of providing community-based care for the first patients discharged is likely to be less than £13,000 per year (because they were the more able) new services have to be developed not just for them but for the others remaining in the community, pushing up costs overall
- The real increase in local authority expenditure on services for the mentally ill, of around £20 million a year over the period, is completely inadequate to meet the likely costs of providing community-based care for the survivors of the 16,800 mentally ill people who were formerly in hospital; and, possibly more important, for those discharged from hospital before becoming long-stay patients. Such services would cost of the order of £240 million a year, on the basis of the two assumptions above, although not all would be provided by local authorities
- Even for mentally handicapped people, there has been little scope for improving the services for clients who were already receiving community-based care in 1976, or whose families would have turned in any event to their local authority's social services department for support.

80. In practice there are a variety of strategies that authorities can adopt to reduce the amount of bridging required for running-down hospitals:

(a) *Closing hospitals in stages.* Where hospitals can be closed in small self-contained units, with most of the overheads also stopping on closure, the bridging peak will be smaller. This option depends on the configuration of existing stock, however, and is largely historically determined. It may be possible to reduce the amount of bridging finance required through careful planning

(b) *Reducing the transition period.* A long drawn-out period of transition gives poor value for money. However, a rapid run-down is not always possible when the health authority is reliant on other agencies as described later in this chapter. Also, speed may work against the interests of individual patients or clients; these may require delay to ensure all is in order before discharge. Reference has already been made to the 15,000 'old long-stay' who may never move into the community

(c) *Adjusting discharge policies.* The set-up and running costs of community services for the most able are much less than the costs for the more dependent. By discharging the least dependent into the community first, overall bridging costs may be reduced. But this approach, too, may clash with professional objectives since it may be thought desirable to place a mixed ability range of patients in the community. Indeed staff of the South East Thames RHA think it essential to discharge patients of a mixed ability range, based on their experience of running-down Darenth Park Hospital.

However, bridging the cost of people coming out of hospital is only part of the story. It is also necessary to set up the services for those following on who do not gain access to long-stay places in the first place under the changed admissions policies.

81. Similarly, the transition costs can be financed by health authorities in a number of different ways:

(a) *Reallocating resources.* It is easier to reallocate resources from other budget heads where the budget is growing. When budgets are static (and even more when they are declining) bridging funds must be generated by diverting money away from services that are no longer required, 'turning the money around' and releasing it for new initiatives. This requires very astute and determined management:

- It appears to be easier to set up new community care developments in areas expanding from a low base (e.g. 'RAWP gainers'), than in relatively well endowed areas where the money is locked up in existing services

- In some authorities visited funds were diverted from other services, with (for example) the opening of an acute unit delayed for some months

- In one authority the Treasurer set up a fund against which the unit managers could borrow, similar to a bank account, with financial 'penalties' for exceeding overdraft limits in the form of reduced capital expenditure. Thus the excesses are funded from capital, reducing and delaying capital schemes, so that managers have an incentive to manage their funds effectively

(b) *Using regional funds.* Most NHS regions have introduced policies for bridging. These policies vary from region to region and for different client groups. Most involve diverting funds from acute care services. Thus the transition costs are funded from development funds or RAWP additions; but in 'RAWP losing' regions the funds available are less than in 'RAWP gaining' regions

(c) *Using joint finance.* This was originally introduced to promote joint planning between agencies. As described above, this provides 'pump priming' money for new schemes; but after a certain time, it tapers off and the bill must be 'picked up' by the main agency responsible. The short-term nature of this source of funds lends itself to bridging purposes. But many authorities are reported to be nervous about using it, in case of delays causing cashflow difficulties when 'pick up' becomes required

(d) *Tapping Supplementary Benefit payments for board and lodging.* If people can be accommodated in facilities where they qualify for board and lodging payments, the cost to the health and local authorities is correspondingly reduced. The bridging finance is thus effectively provided by Supplementary Benefit. This can have a distorting effect on patterns of care for individual clients, since types of care that qualify for support from Supplementary Benefits may be preferred over more suitable (and probably lower costs) alternatives which do not attract benefits. This is discussed further below

(e) *Selling and leasing back the hospital site.* Many mental hospitals occupy valuable sites (though many, of course, do not). Preliminary estimates by the Commission based on tentative information from some regions suggest that the resale value of the existing mental hospitals could be of the order of £500 million – concentrated in those regions (in London and the South East) which are tending to lose under the RAWP arrangements. In principal, when land could be developed for residential housing, there would be much to be said for a straightforward sale and lease-back arrangement. The interest on the sale proceeds would, in effect, help to fund the transition costs incurred by the NHS. However, such arrangements would have implications for the control of public expenditure.

82. These various devices provide treasurers with a range of options. Nonetheless, it is apparent that the bridging funds available are inadequate in many areas, and particularly where large hospitals for both mentally handicapped and mentally ill people are being run down at the same time. Lack of funds to cover set-up costs in the community appears to be a particular problem.

Capital Implications

83. In addition to the need for revenue bridging funds, additional capital may be required during the transition period. As with revenue, each agency has its own source of capital, with the amount available separately determined. In health authorities, community care schemes have to compete with other priorities – with hospitals, health centres etc; and in local authority housing departments where maintenance and improvement works, of which there is a £20 billion backlog, virtually preclude new building (ref. 16).

84. Just as different models of care have different revenue consequences, some models of care may be more capital-intensive than others. Models requiring purpose-built facilities are generally more capital intensive. Furthermore, concepts of community care are changing so fast that buildings are often needed for only a relatively short time before being overtaken by new initiatives. As recently as five years ago, units for mentally handicapped people with more than 80 beds were being considered; but now much smaller units – perhaps a terraced house with four to five residents, or a single household supported by a 'flying squad' are preferred. So, some 80-bed units now approaching completion will be out of date before they open. Flexibility appears to be key. In several authorities, relatively new purpose-built facilities for mentally handicapped people are being converted for other client groups (principally elderly mentally ill people) and replaced by smaller units – usually houses purchased on the open market.

85. It is impossible to identify precisely the amount of capital required to ensure that community care proceeds. This will depend on the stock already available, the model of care adopted, and the local costs of land and buildings. This information is not yet available. However, as with revenue, the rules governing the availability of capital vary between agencies and cannot take into account the specific needs of individual community care programmes. This fragmentation and inflexibility is once again likely to hamper rather than promote good value for money; and it could well distort and delay the introduction of community care. Methods for allowing greater flexibility at the local level could overcome some of these difficulties, as the Commission pointed out in its report *Capital Expenditure Controls in Local Government in England* (ref. 17).

86. Housing associations offer an alternative at a time when the need for community housing for priority groups is rising, and local authorities have seen their overall housing investment programme allocations reduced by 50% in real terms since 1979. However, there has been a dramatic reduction in local authority lending to housing associations, to about a quarter of the level prevailing only a few years ago. As a result, with a few notable exceptions, housing associations rely on the Housing Corporation for finance. But the possibility of tapping building society funds for housing associations would seem to have considerable potential as a way of bridging any shortfall in capital for housing in the community. In one authority a housing association had raised funds on the open market from a building society; and the loan was guaranteed by the local authority in exchange for 100% allocation rights.

PERVERSE EFFECTS OF SOCIAL SECURITY POLICIES

87. Social security payments have played a major part in promoting care in the community. The range of benefits that is relevant to the priority groups are described in Appendix C. Most of these benefits provide income support or help to meet normal accommodation costs. The three benefits that are most relevant to meeting the cost of caring for the ill or disabled are the Attendance Allowance, the Invalid Care Allowance and the Supplementary Benefit payments for board and lodging (independent homes):

(a) Attendance Allowance is payable at one of two rates (see below) to people aged two and over who by virtue of mental or physical disablement are, and have been for at least 6 months before an award is made, in need of:

– Frequent attention throughout the day in connection with their bodily functions, or

– Continual supervision throughout the day to avoid substantial danger to themselves or others

– Prolonged or repeated attention at night, or

– Continual supervision at night to avoid substantial danger to themselves or others.

The higher rate which is currently £30.95 per week, is payable to those who satisfy a day *and* night condition; the lower rate currently £20.65, to those satisfying either the day *or* night condition. The Allowance is not means-tested.

(b) The Invalid Care Allowance is for those who give up work to care for an invalid living in their own home. It is payable at a rate of £23.25 per week. It is not means-tested and is separate from Attendance Allowance which is payable to the disabled person. Beneficiaries must be caring for someone who is in receipt of the Attendance Allowance or Constant Attendance Allowance, for at least 35 hours per week; and their earnings must not exceed £12 per week

(c) Supplementary Benefit payments for board and lodging (independent homes) are payable to those in private or voluntary residential care homes or nursing homes. It is means-tested. The maximum rate payable varies from £125 per week to £230 per week, depending on the level of care provided. An extension of £17.50 per week to these rates is payable within Greater London. In more detail, the weekly limits applying to residential care homes and nursing homes outside of Greater London from July 1986 are as follows:

Table 17: SUPPLEMENTARY BENEFIT PAYMENTS FOR BOARD AND LODGING (INDEPENDENT HOMES) – MAXIMUM LIMITS OUTSIDE LONDON

	Residential	Nursing
Physically Disabled (incurred below pension age)	£180 per week	230
Mentally Handicapped	150	200
Very Dependent Elderly	140	170
Drug or Alcohol Dependent	130	180
Mentally Ill	130	180
Elderly or Other	125	170

People in hospices and other homes caring for the terminally ill can claim up to £230 per week. The special rate for very dependent elderly introduced in July 1986 applies only to residents who are blind, or who qualify for the higher rate Attendance Allowance. The payment is means tested according to Supplementary Benefit rules. Thus it is only payable to those with savings of less than £3,000, and most sources of income are deducted from the allowance payable (see Appendix C for a more detailed description).

88. However, in contrast to Attendance Allowance and Invalid Care Allowance no test of degree of disability is required for Supplementary Benefit payments for board and lodging unless the special rate for 'very dependent elderly' is being claimed. Thus, anybody fulfilling the Supplementary Benefit rules (irrespective of the extent of disability) who chooses to live in a residential home is entitled to allowances meeting their full fees up to £125 or more a week — considerably more than Attendance Allowance and Invalid Care Allowance combined, although some of the difference is accounted for by accommodation costs, for which separate benefits are available in the community. Indeed, paradoxically, many people fulfilling the conditions for Attendance and Invalid Care Allowances would be too disabled to be cared for adequately in a residential home. In these circumstances the temptation must be strong for anyone trying to look after a relative at home to make use of the more generous, and far less stringent, payments for board and lodging, by placing them in residential care.

89. In short, the more residential the care, the easier it is to obtain benefits, and the greater the size of the payment. And Supplementary Benefit funding cannot be targeted towards those individuals most in need of residential care. Nor are homes judged on whether they are giving value for money within the category of care for which they are registered. A Joint Working Party (ref. 18) recommended that pilot studies should be undertaken of the multi-disciplinary assessment of Supplementary Benefit claimants in independent homes. These are currently being undertaken through the Social Policy Research Unit at York University. In the meantime, very large sums of public money are being paid to people living in private homes without there being any mechanism (other than means-testing income) for ensuring that the benefits are appropriate. In fact, a recent study by the Association of Directors of Social Services entitled *Who goes Where* (ref. 19) found that 'the statistics consistently indicate that residents at the time of admission in local authority homes are more frail than those in private homes'. Furthermore, the Commission's own findings (ref.10) suggest that many in local authority homes do not need to be there: 'in three authorities studied in detail about half of the residents in the authorities' homes could have been supported in the community had the necessary resources been available.'

90. Thus social security policies appear to be working in a way directly opposing community care policies. Furthermore, this situation is becoming more acute. The latest DHSS estimates of the number of claimants and cost of these three allowances in 1984–5 is shown below.

Table 18:   LATEST DHSS ESTIMATES OF SOCIAL SECURITY BENEFITS
Great Britain 1984–5

	Beneficiaries	Annual Cost
Supplementary Benefits Payments for Board and Lodging (indep. homes)	42,000	£200m
Attendance Allowance	543,000	576
Invalid Care Allowance	9,500	11

The number of claimants for Invalid Care Allowance is likely to rise sharply in the near future following the recent change in rules to include married women. Expenditure on the community-based Attendance Allowance has been rising steadily as Exhibit 11 shows. But expenditure on Supplementary Benefit payments for board and lodging (independent homes) by contrast has been increasing at an exponential rate. DHSS estimate that over the period December 1981 to December 1984 expenditure was more than

Exhibit 11

TRENDS IN SOCIAL SECURITY PAYMENTS, 1976-86

Great Britain

£m at November 1986 prices

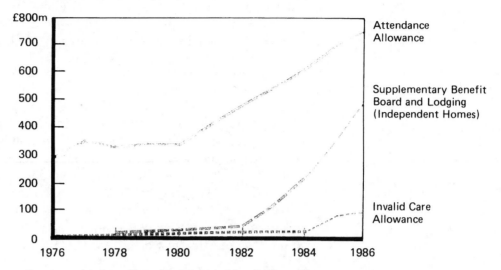

Sources: (a) Attendance Allowance and Invalid Care Allowance:
Social Security Statistics 1985 and 1986 Public
Expenditure White Paper Cmnd 9789 (see Appendix C)

(b) Supplementary Benefit Board and Lodging
(Independent Homes): DHSS figures to 1984;
Audit Commission Survey for 1985 and 1986 (see
Appendix D)

doubling annually. Analysis based on the Audit Commission's survey
(Appendix D) indicates that the number of claimants will have doubled again
between December 1984 and the end of 1986, to 85,000 costing £500 million a
year in Supplementary Benefit payments.

91. There is, therefore, risk of serious distortion of public expenditure
priorities, because there are two parallel systems of public financing of
people in residential homes who are unable to meet their own expenses.
Local authorities are becoming increasingly aware that board and lodging
payments can often meet the accommodation and care costs of those in
independent homes who might previously have been sponsored by the local
authority. In at least two of the authorities visited, a 'gain' of £1 million a year
(each) had been received by transferring to Supplementary Benefits
responsibility for people placed in voluntary sector residential
accommodation. Furthermore, health and local authorities are using
Supplementary Benefit payments for board and lodging to reduce their
expenditure on residential and in-patient care, by transferring some of their
own homes to private management so that eligible residents can claim
Supplementary Benefit to help meet the fees. There is considerable potential
for further transfers – with the theoretical upper limit of £2 billion provided
by the (admittedly, highly unlikely) combination of:

- Nearly all residents qualifying for Supplementary Benefits
- All residents of local authority homes (and those supported by
  local authorities in independent homes) 'privatised' with a cost to
  Supplementary Benefits, which could cost an *additional* £800
  million a year
- All geriatric in-patients and those in mental health hospitals are
  similarly 'transferred' to privately-managed nursing homes, with a
  net transfer of an additional £1.5 billion a year of expenditure from
  the NHS to Supplementary Benefits.

Such transfers are tempting to hard-pressed managers. But unlike the community care policies, they increase the public sector borrowing requirement as Supplementary Benefit payments are not cash-limited. And, of course, they confirm people in residential care settings.

92. Finally, Supplementary Benefit claimants are very unevenly distributed across the country. Regional variations occur because private homes are not evenly distributed, but concentrated in former holiday areas – particularly the South Coast with more places available per head of population of people aged over 75 than in other areas. Exhibit 7 showed this uneven distribution. This concentration is undermining the effect of any 'fine tuning' between areas through RAWP and the Rate Support Grant, and channelling public funds to people in some of the better off, least deprived parts of the country. Table 19 compares the effect of the public funds spent on different regions, of RAWP and of increases in payments for board and lodging. It is apparent that the effect of the Supplementary Benefit payments is to change the 'winners' and 'losers' quite substantially. Yet RAWP has been the subject of the closest analysis and intensive political and professional debate; whereas the way the Supplementary Benefit payments have been distributed has 'just happened'. Moreover, these payments are continuing to grow rapidly, and are not subject to any central control either in total or in the way in which they are distributed across the country.

Table 19: EFFECT OF RAWP AND CHANGES IN SB PAYMENTS, 1977–85
£ per person

NHS Regions	NHS (RAWP) Gain	Board and Lodging	Net Gain
North Western	£36.11 per person	5.87	41.98
Northern	32.71	3.22	35.93
Trent	29.37	3.75	33.12
Mersey	28.83	5.33	34.16
South Western	26.44	13.28	39.72
Wessex	24.98	11.36	36.34
East Anglian	24.73	7.56	32.29
Yorkshire	24.05	5.72	29.77
West Midlands	24.00	4.22	28.22
SW Thames	20.33	10.69	31.02
NE Thames	16.72	4.19	20.91
SE Thames	10.27	9.31	19.58
NW Thames	7.88	4.63	12.51
Oxford	5.49	5.42	10.91

93. In summary, Supplementary Benefit payments are an increasingly important source of funds for care, but they are not controlled by either health or local authorities; and they may be working against the community care initiative:

- They are placing an undue emphasis on residential care, where other services may be more suitable for the client and cost less
- They are distorting the distribution of funds across the country
- While there are mechanisms (however inadequate) for transferring and redirecting funds from health authorities to local government, no such mechanisms exist for linking social security funds and policies to local initiatives in any way. Instead, health and local authorities must adjust their policies to produce 'social security efficient' schemes, which favour more expensive residential care over the community-based services
- The total of public funds available in an area is in effect determined arbitrarily: health, local authority and social security funds depend on different formulae and demands. The result is that public

expenditure is not necessarily focused on the areas and/or clients where the need for support is greatest.

94. The effects of the conflicts between social security, NHS and local authority funding priorities can be illustrated best by looking at some case examples. Two theoretical examples illustrate the financial implications of different modes of care:

- The first involves a frail elderly single person on state pension without substantial savings. Such a person could be supported in a number of alternative ways (and studies have shown that people supported in hospital, residential care, and the community often have similar characteristics). The alternatives evaluated are as follows:

  (i) Own home with domiciliary support (with some home help, meals and a visit from a community nurse each week)

  (ii) As above but with day care also included

  (iii) As above but the person's own home is in local authority sheltered housing

  (iv) In local authority part III home

  (v) In private or voluntary residential accommodation

  (vi) In private or voluntary nursing home

  (vii) In hospital (NHS geriatric ward).

- The second example is for a mentally handicapped person qualifying for Severe Disablement Allowance. The alternative forms of accommodation evaluated here (with associated day and domiciliary services as appropriate) are:

  (a) In own home alone

  (b) In a local authority group home

  (c) In lodgings supported by a landlady

  (d) In a local authority residential home

  (e) In a private or voluntary residential home

  (f) In a mental handicap hospital.

95. Table 20 overleaf shows an illustrative set of costs to the public purse of the alternative modes of care for the frail single elderly person, and the costs to each agency. To make the costs strictly comparable, the opportunity costs of the property should also be added for local authority residential homes and the NHS hospital (the revenue equivalent of the market value for the properties per place – say £10 – 20 extra per week). Table 21 overleaf provides the same information for the example of the mentally handicapped person (the same caveat on capital applies).

96. Three main conclusions can be drawn. First, costs to the public purse in these alternative patterns of care range from under £100 a week to nearly £300 a week. Second, the cost to individual agencies varies enormously. And third, the cost to an individual agency bears no relation to the cost to the public purse overall. Thus, if one agency sets out to minimise its cost, the result may be a more expensive option for the taxpayer overall. In fact, if a social services department seeks to minimise its costs, the more expensive residential options overall to the public purse are chosen – private or voluntary home or hospital. Perversely, money is available for some of the high cost institutional options, while the low cost options are starved of finance. In such circumstances, it is small wonder that progress with community care has been both slow and uneven.

Table 20: COST OF ALTERNATIVE PACKAGES OF CARE FOR AN ELDERLY PERSON ILLUSTRATIVE

Frail elderly single person on state pension (without substantial savings). Qualifying for Attendance Allowance at lower rate. Disability incurred after retirement age. Long-term costs per week.

	(i) Own Home	(ii) Own Home +Day Care	(iii) LA Sheltered Housing	(iv) LA Part III Home	(v) P&V* Residential Home	(vi) P&V* Nursing Home	(vii) NHS Geriatric Ward
Cost to Social Security							
State Pension	£38.70 p/w	38.70	38.70	38.70	38.70	38.70	7.75
Certificated Housing Benefit	19.00	19.00	30.00	–	–	–	–
Attendance Allowance	20.65	20.65	20.65	–	20.65	20.65	–
Supplementary Benefit	1.40	1.40	1.40	–	74.70	119.70	–
Costs to NHS							
Home Care	4.00	4.00	4.00	–	–	–	–
In-Patient Care	–	–	–	–	–	–	287.00
Costs to Personal Social Services							
Domiciliary Services	12.00	12.00	12.00	–	–	–	–
Day Centre	–	38.00	38.00	–	–	–	–
Residential Care (net)	–	–	–	90.05	–	–	–
Costs to Housing Dept							
Housing Revenue Account Deficit on Sheltered Housing	–	–	5.20	–	–	–	–
Cost to DOE							
Rate Relief	1.60	1.60	1.60	4.50	4.50	4.50	–
Costs by Agency							
Social Security	79.75	79.75	90.75	38.70	134.05	179.05	7.75
NHS	4.00	4.00	4.00	–	–	–	287.00
Personal Social Services	12.00	50.00	50.00	90.05	–	–	–
Housing Department	–	–	5.20	–	–	–	–
DOE	1.60	1.60	1.60	4.50	4.50	4.50	–
Total Public Cost	97.35	135.35	151.55	133.25	138.55	183.55	294.75

* Private and voluntary

Table 21: COST OF ALTERNATIVE PACKAGES OF CARE FOR A MENTALLY HANDICAPPED PERSON ILLUSTRATIVE

Mentally Handicapped Adult. Qualifying for Severe Disablement Allowance but not Attendance Allowance or Invalid Care Allowance. No savings or other income. Long-term costs per week.

	(a) Own Home alone	(b) LA Group Home (four people)	(c) Sup. Ben. Supported Lodging	(d) LA Residential Home	(e) P&V* Residential Home	(f) Mental Handicap Hospital
Cost to Social Security						
Severe Disablement Allowance	£23.25 p/w	23.25	23.25	23.25	23.25	7.75
Supplementary Benefit	14.65	11.91	57.70	15.45	135.80	–
Housing Benefit	19.00	14.00	–	–	–	–
Cost to NHS						
In-patient Care	–	–	–	–	–	247.00
Cost to Personal Social Services						
Domiciliary	28.00	8.00	4.00	–	–	–
Training Centre	46.00	46.00	46.00	46.00	46.00	–
Residential Care	–	14.00	–	101.05	–	–
Cost to DOE						
Rate Relief	1.60	1.60	1.60	4.50	4.50	–
Costs by Agency						
Social Security	56.90	49.16	80.95	38.70	159.05	7.75
NHS	–	–	–	–	–	247.00
Personal Social Services	74.00	68.00	50.00	147.05	46.00	–
DOE	1.60	1.60	1.60	4.50	4.50	–
Total Public Cost	132.50	118.76	132.55	190.25	209.55	254.75

* Private and voluntary

**ORGANISATIONAL
FRAGMENTATION
AND CONFUSION**

97. Conflicting policies are in large part a result of the division of responsibility for the implementation of community care between separate government departments: the Department of Environment and the health and social security sides of DHSS. A similar degree of organisational fragmentation is encountered at the more local level:

- Residential care usually involves only one agency – either health (hospital or nursing home), the private or voluntary sectors (nursing or residential homes), or social services (residential homes). Most services are provided under one roof and are co-ordinated by the person in charge, simplifying administrative arrangements.

- By contrast, care in the community for an individual may well involve services from a number of agencies or voluntary organisations at the same time, in addition to care provided by family and friends. Thus a recipient of care in the community may be housed in sheltered housing provided by the housing department, attend a day centre provided by the social services department, and receive visits at home from the home help service (social services) nursing services (NHS) and a care attendant scheme (voluntary sector). Without some part of this 'package of care' it may be impossible for the client to remain in the community at all.

Exhibit 12 overleaf shows these agencies and the relationships between them, and Exhibit 13 overleaf summarises the contribution made by each agency.

98. These services must 'mesh' if community care is to work. In particular, services must be provided in suitable amounts, requiring sound 'service planning'; and they must be made available to individual people in appropriate 'packages', requiring effective 'operational planning'. Unfortunately the present management arrangements do not promote the essential integrated service and operational planning. In particular:

(i) The structure of local community-based services is confused, with responsibility and accountability for elements of the services fragmented between different tiers of the NHS and within local government.

(ii) As a result, the joint planning arrangements need to be complex and are particularly time-consuming to operate to ensure adequate liaison between all the various interests involved.

(iii) The difficulties posed by the confused structure and complex planning arrangements are compounded by the lack of incentives and differences in the organisation styles of the different agencies concerned.

Each of these problems might be soluble in isolation; but, together, they have combined to make it extraordinarily difficult to manage the transition to community-based care at the local level.

**Confused Structure and
Fragmented
Accountability**

99. The structural problems arise at three levels: national, regional and local. The national problems have already been referred to. The difficulties arising at the regional and local levels are, if anything, even more acute. And the most serious difficulties arise at the operational level. Each warrants separate mention.

*Problems at the national
level*

100. At the national level the extent to which the detailed implementation of community care policies can be directed from the centre is necessarily limited. The Government has recognised and acknowledged these limits in its reply to the Third Report, Session 1979–80 of the House of Commons Select Committee on Social Services:

'The Government see their role as essentially strategic. They have

Exhibit 12

PRINCIPAL AGENCIES INVOLVED IN COMMUNITY CARE

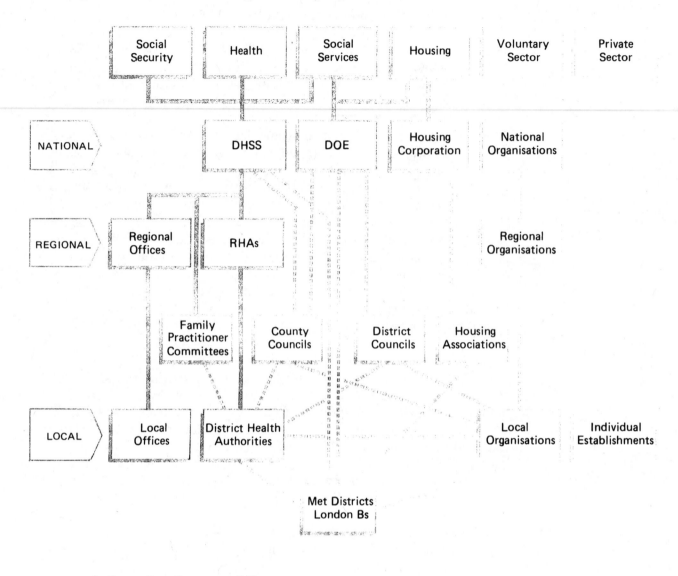

Indicates direct line responsibility

Indicates interrelationship

Exhibit 13

MAIN CARE AND ACCOMMODATION SERVICES

AGENCY	FORM OF CARE	SERVICE	VARIATIONS
Health Authorities	Hospitals	— In-patients	— Long-stay — Short-stay/respite
	Residential	— Day — Community units — Nursing homes	
	Community Services	— Nurses	— Qualified — Auxiliary
		— Health visitors — Therapists	— Physiotherapists — Chiropody
Family Practitioner Committees	Primary Health Care	— GPs — Nurses — Dental and opthalmic services	
Social Services	Residential	— Residential homes	— Long-stay — Short-stay/respite
	Accommodation	— Staffed group homes — Unstaffed group homes — Sheltered lodgings	
	Day Care	— Workshops — Day centres — Training centres — Drop-in centres	
	Domiciliary	— Social workers — Good neighbours — Home helps — Therapists	— Occupational
Housing Authorities	Housing	— Sheltered housing	— Wardens — Alarm systems
		— Hostels — Group homes — Flats/houses	— Improvement grants
Education	Training facilities for adults		
Voluntary Sector and Housing Associations	Residential Housing	— Residential homes — Group homes — Sheltered housing — Flats/houses	— For special needs
	Day Care	— Luncheon clubs — Drop-in centres	
	Domiciliary	— Care attendant schemes — Volunteers/good neighbours	
Private Sector	Residential	— Nursing homes — Residential homes	
	Housing Domiciliary	— Sheltered housing — Domestic agencies	

responsibility for the level of funding of the NHS and Ministers will continue to give strategic guidance relating to national policies and priorities, broadly indicating ways in which they look for development in the Service and where economies should be sought. But if the Government's policy of giving greater responsibility to the new district health authorities is to be effective, it is essential that those authorities should have adequate flexibility in applying national guidelines in a way that takes proper account of local needs and circumstances. In the case of management costs specific limits have been set; in general, however, guidance will be less detailed and precise than in the past.'

This thinking is in line with some of the best management thinking at the present time with authority delegated as far as possible.

101. However, the Government has been prescriptive about several matters which might more appropriately be decided closer to patients:

- There seems little to be gained by trying to control manpower targets as well as finance. Community care is almost always more labour intensive and limits on manpower numbers could lead to inefficiencies as closure of older high cost (but lower manpower) services is delayed because lower cost, more labour intensive domiciliary services cannot be introduced
- The *Land Transactions Handbook* for Health Authorities prescribes and limits activities of managers, preventing the flexibility necessary when introducing care in the community. One inner London health authority complained of difficulties in using its former staff houses effectively, because of requirements imposed by the Handbook – increasing the possibility of placing a greater load on the local housing authority
- The DHSS is also very prescriptive about how authorities should plan. The draft circular (ref. 20) issued in January 1986 was thought by many authorities to be too prescriptive and to give too little scope to managers to work out the most appropriate arrangements to meet local requirements.

It is generally more effective to monitor 'outputs' (progress towards community care) rather than 'inputs' (staff, property, planning machinery), even if the latter is generally easier to measure.

Problems at the regional level

102. In England, there is no organisation at regional level for local government. On the other hand, RHAs play a significant role in the planning process. But there is a danger that they may frustrate the move to community care, because they have only a limited contact with local authorities and they play a more direct role in the closure of hospitals than in the build-up of alternatives in the community.

103. RHAs' limited contact with local authorities means that proposals and developments may be made which do not take account of the local authority perspective. In some of the authorities visited it was apparent that the relations between local authorities and RHAs were poor. Councils complain that the RHAs ignored them; and the RHAs assert that all directors of social services do is to complain about money. It is not difficult to see how these problems arise. The regional plans set out timetables for closure of large hospitals; but these have generally not been negotiated with local authorities, even though they have a major and direct impact on them. This is because closure of such hospitals may affect several different local authorities, and regions need to take a lead if any progress is to be made. The draft circular on joint planning proposes closer working relations between RHAs and local authorities. But there is a serious risk that such a link will by-pass and undermine relations with district health authorities. In addition

the method of working is different, with 'top down' planning from RHAs to districts in the health service, and 'bottom up' planning from individual authorities in local government.

104. In addition, although regions are often directly involved in drawing up plans for the closure of hospitals, they are less involved in the build-up of alternative services. These remain the responsibility of health districts, and local authorities. Where people are discharged from long-stay hospitals, the RHAs are often directly involved in ensuring that the placement is appropriate – sometimes before agreeing that transfer payments can be made. However, the region is only indirectly involved in the build-up of community-based services not directly linked with discharges from long-stay hospitals – through the approval of district health authority plans. And RHAs are not at all involved in the provisions of community-based services by local authorities. So, while the English RHAs are in a strong position to influence the run-down of hospital facilities, they are not in a position to ensure the build-up of suitable alternatives in the community.

105. If community care is to work these two initiatives must be kept in balance. But, there are powerful forces pushing for hospital closures, without corresponding forces pushing for the development of alternatives in the community. The reduction and closure of beds in hospitals for mentally handicapped and mentally ill people is the subject of targets in some regions for the management reviews introduced following the introduction of 'Griffiths' management in 1984. Management performance will be assessed against these targets, with the renewal of short term contracts for general managers possibly at stake. Moreover, there are powerful financial arguments for pressing ahead and closing hospitals as rapidly as possible:

- It is more expensive to run hospital *and* community facilities in parallel, and bridging finance is required (as described earlier in this chapter)
- Considerable difficulties are encountered in managing a hospital threatened with closure, including keeping up morale and standards, and retaining adequate staff.

Monitoring the build-up of suitable alternatives is more difficult than following progress in closing hospitals – because the measures are much less clear cut.

106. As a result, there is a danger that the run-down of hospital beds will continue to occur ahead of the build-up of alternative facilities. Whilst those discharged from hospital may be properly cared for there is no guarantee of suitable packages of care for the 'cohorts' that will follow. This need not be the case, as experience shows in Wales, where the Welsh Office has a more extensive role than English RHAs. As well as fulfilling the role of RHA, the Welsh Office also has an influence over local authorities – including both social services and housing. This gives the Welsh Office an opportunity to switch money between budget heads, thus overcoming the difficulties of separate funding. In addition, 'All-Wales' strategies – first for mentally handicapped people (ref. 21) and subsequently for elderly people (ref. 22) have provided the framework for implementing community care. In the case of services for mentally handicapped people, considerable sums have been made available to 'bridge' community care services *before* hospital services are run down. This approach is leading to worthwhile progress (ref. 23).

Problems at the local level

107. As Exhibit 12 showed, the organisational arrangements for delivering care in the community reach their most complex at the local level. The various agencies must work together, undertaking both service and operational planning. The working arrangements can take several forms:

(a) Sub-contracting, where one agency has responsibility for the delivery of the service and 'buys-in' skills and services from other agencies. The responsible agency controls the budget

(b) Provision of services 'on demand', where one agency or individual can demand services of another, and the second is obliged by law to meet this demand. Examples include the provision of social security payments to people meeting the eligibility criteria laid down; the committal of children into the care of local authorities by the Courts; and the housing of homeless families

(c) Voluntary co-operation, where one agency may request action or service from another which may then supply the service from its own budget. The supplying agency is under no obligation to do so, other than a desire to provide appropriate services to the client

(d) Go-it-alone. The agency requiring a service can decide to extend its own provision of services to provide the required service in-house.

108. At least two of these working arrangements – (b) and (c) – are less than satisfactory from a management point of view. Managers cannot sensibly be held to account for the quality of the service they provide if they must depend on the voluntary co-operation of another independent agency to provide it. And yet, most of the agencies involved in community care relate to each other in this way. Similarly, managers who have no control over the demand for their services cannot be held responsible for meeting this demand unless they have an open-ended budget, which is the antithesis of managerial accountability.

109. In addition, the different agencies involved in providing community-based care have different priorities.

Health: Acute services. While priority groups are, by definition, to receive priority, the provision of acute services is by far the largest and most important role of district health authorities. Much of the growth in priority services is being funded from efficiency savings in the acute sector, and if these savings are not forthcoming, plans for the priority groups may be delayed.

Social services: Child care services. Recently there has been increasing legislation on children's services adding to workloads without there being any corresponding increases in staff. Taken together with tighter procedures following recent child care scandals, priority given to child care work reduces the effort available for community care.

Housing: Homeless people. Housing departments have a statutory duty to secure accommodation (not necessarily in council stock) for homeless families and homeless vulnerable people (who include disabled and mentally ill people), and to give these and other homeless people along with certain other groups 'a reasonable preference' in selecting council tenants (section 22 of the *Housing Act* 1985).

Voluntary agencies: Different roles. Many voluntary agencies are torn between being 'service providers' and being 'pressure groups'. The two roles are not easily compatible. Being a service provider involves co-operation and collaboration; being a pressure group involves challenge and confrontation.

Private sector: Return on investment. The private sector has a need to realise a return on investment. The greater the care given, the higher the costs. With a maximum weekly rate from Supplementary Benefits charge from social security there is a financial incentive to take less dependent people who do not require much care.

110. This strategic divergence must be set against the day-to-day convergence between the services provided by the health service and local authority personal social services departments:

- Health authorities have been reducing lengths of stay in hospitals and discharging into the community people who previously would have been in-patients (costing nearly £300 per week) for long periods
- Local authority residential homes have been taking increasingly disabled residents over the years and now look after people who would formerly have been in hospital
- Home help services are increasingly becoming 'home care' services, overlapping with community nursing services
- Day centres, with increasingly frail and disabled clients and their increasing emphasis on rehabilitation, are becoming more like day hospitals
- District council housing departments are increasingly becoming involved in community care and some are expanding their involvement through alarm systems, mobile wardens, improvement grants, and welfare officers. One housing manager felt that it was quite wrong to view housing departments as simply being 'managers of bricks and mortar' and that they have a key role in advising and helping people.

111. This convergence increases the difficulties caused by the fragmented organisation and the failure of joint planning to resolve them. Indeed, at the local level, confusion may occur between agencies as to who is doing what. In particular, domiciliary services for elderly people may include auxiliary nurses (health services), home helps (social services), mobile wardens (housing) and care attendants (voluntary sector). The different roles of these various different staff may well overlap. Conversely, gaps may occur for example between services for elderly mentally ill people, with health staff arguing that such elderly people do not require continuing medical care in hospitals, and social services staff arguing that such people are acutely mentally ill and beyond their responsibilities.

Problems at the operational level

112. In addition to an integrated range of services, community care also requires that the people responsible for operating the system also work together, to ensure that individuals are properly assessed, and economic and balanced packages of services are provided that best fit their needs. Operational planning is the responsibility of the many professionals at the 'front line'. These include:

- Doctors (GPs, consultants)
- Nurses
- Health visitors
- Social workers (field, day and residential)
- Home care organisers
- Occupational therapists
- Physiotherapists
- Psychologists
- Housing managers
- Social security officers.

Each has a different background, training and perspective. Care professionals traditionally act as independent practitioners, which can hamper attempts to co-ordinate community care. Thus in parallel with organisational and financial fragmentation, there can be a danger of 'professional fragmentation'.

113. One example is given by the way in which the primary health care team – and in particular GPs – relate to community care services. In theory they are complementary, with the primary health care team sorting out the medical issues; and the community care team sorting out such items as accommodation, rehabilitation and training, care and support. In practice the boundary is less clear cut. For example there is a potential conflict of interests for nurses, whose role straddles both services, although they are often based in primary health care teams. A comparison of different methods of organising the work of community psychiatric nurses suggests that where they are attached to general practices rather than remaining part of multidisciplinary psychiatric teams, the time spent with people chronically disabled by severe psychiatric disorders such as schizoprenia is markedly diminished and a new (less disabled) clientele is taken on (see ref. 24). In practice considerable tensions can exist between primary health care teams and community care services – particularly where resources are short.

114. Some of these tensions can lead to delay in progressing community care. While most people agree that community care is the right way forward, there has been less ready agreement on the form that community care should take. There has been opposition and delay by professionals who feel that their interests, and the interests of clients and patients are threatened.

115. There has also been opposition from the general public. Many people introducing services in the community described the need to spend great amounts of time on public relations. Exeter Health Authority has even developed a video explaining the implications of new services. The White Paper *Better Services for the Mentally Ill* drew attention to the need to ensure that 'the demands which different groups of ill or disabled people make in total upon the community must not be greater than the community can accept'. However, except in a few progressive authorities there was little risk of overloading the community. The problem was rather one of a lack of any significant progress towards the introduction of community care at all.

*   *   *

116. The result of this confusion, inevitably, is frustration. This word was used time and again by staff wanting to get on with the job, but being frustrated by the system – blocked by another agency working to different priorities and different time scales; or by a lack of money for a new scheme that would advance community care. One of the results of such frustration is often that people start to move in on other people's responsibilities, possibly adopting a 'go-it-alone' strategy. Such moves heighten the confusion, with people tackling jobs that should not be theirs (according to the organisational chart) and neglecting jobs that are. This can (and often does) occur at all levels, blurring responsibility and accountability even further.

Complex Joint Planning Arrangements

117. Since the progress of community care depends upon the mutual agreement and concerted action of a number of independent separately funded agencies that can only 'request' services of each other, effective joint planning machinery is essential. At the hub of the present local planning machinery is the joint consultative committee (JCC), made up of members of the health authority and social services committee with representatives from housing, education, family practitioner committees and the voluntary sector who add a valuable extra dimension. In general the committee is served by an officer group called the joint care planning team (JCPT). Serving this is a network of sub-committees usually concerned with planning services for individual client groups.

118. There are a number of difficulties inherent in placing responsibility for progressing community care on such a mechanism. Many of these have been well documented elsewhere – for example in *Progress in Partnership* (ref. 25). If one of the agencies involved does not (or cannot) co-operate, at best any subsequent action will be delayed or distorted with key elements missing; at worst, there will be no action at all. Such ragged or disjointed progress was one of the most common features observed:

- In one area visited, a carefully scheduled programme for the closure of hospitals for mentally handicapped people was delayed by years because the local housing department could not provide suitable housing for the accommodation of people discharged from hospital

- In a second health authority which related to two district councils, one housing department was providing housing for both mentally ill and handicapped people and sheltered housing for elderly people; the other was very reluctant to provide any housing for priority groups. A distorted pattern was emerging with one half of the authority accommodating all the priority groups

- In a third case, the local director of social services could secure no co-operation from the health authority through the service planning machinery

- In a fourth instance, the health authority general manager had set up excellent community based services including residential homes and group homes almost totally by-passing the social services department.

119. This pattern is well known and is not at all surprising. Part of the difficulty relates to logistics. The number of joint meetings that must be attended is very large and can stretch management staff severely. The director of social services of one of the largest shire counties estimated that his staff have to attend 2,000 such meetings each year; at the national level, it is entirely possible that the existing joint planning machinery costs of the order of £10 million a year in senior staff time alone.

120. The greater the number of agencies that must be involved and the greater the difference in the style, structures and systems of the various agencies, the less likely it must be that agreement will be reached – because the chances of somebody disagreeing will be increased. Even where agreement is reached, if many different people are involved, the agreement may be based on the 'lowest common denominator' rather than the most effective, efficient and economic solution. Solutions thus tend to be piecemeal, since comprehensive change is more difficult to agree.

121. Of course, the problems in joint planning are greatest where health, housing and social services boundaries do not coincide. The so-called 'co-terminosity problem' is well known and often quoted (see for example *Progress in Partnership*). It is particularly acute in central London. Exhibit 14 overleaf shows the position in a large shire county; the potential problems in securing co-ordinated and timely action are obvious.

Differences in Style and Incentives

122. Where agencies are very different there is occasional 'culture shock' between them. Such difficulties were observed in a number of situations. Since 1982 health authorities have been operating the 'Griffiths' style of management, under which general managers have budgets and authority to take decisions. Local authority staff have no such delegated authority, and must continually refer decisions to their respective committees. There were a number of complaints that 'local authorities cannot commit' – particularly the staff involved in joint planning. Often plans are agreed in joint planning forums only to be overturned in committee. Frustration on both sides with this arrangement was considerable.

Exhibit 14

AUTHORITIES INVOLVED IN COMMUNITY CARE

Example: Devon

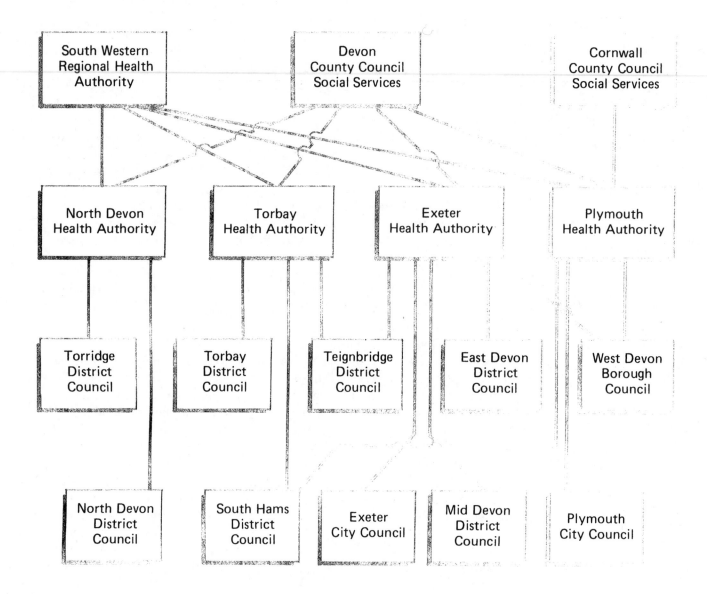

123. A further example of the clash of styles is given by the different timetables operated by the different agencies. General managers appointed under the Griffiths arrangements are on short-term contracts and are in a hurry. Given the choice of doing things quickly or waiting and doing them more effectively, the temptation may be to go for expediency rather than suitability. Thus in one authority, the health service is building a network of nursing homes, and requested sites of the local authority. Rather than wait for sufficient suitable sites, there were proposals to build two homes on one site to save time. This situation was resolved in time when an alternative site in an adjacent neighbourhood was found; but different timetables of this sort can cause friction and undermine joint planning.

124. Moreover, difficulties can occur when the different agencies represented on the JCC are of different political persuasions. In one area visited, the main district council (housing) and the county council (social services) were run by different political parties who could not agree on anything let alone joint strategies.

125. Further problems arise over charging policies. Social services charge for services while health authorities do not. This can cause major difficulties with people resentful of paying for one (local authority) service, when well aware of a very similar free (health) service. Another comment received was that health authorities are too 'bed orientated', and tend to match hospital beds reduced as part of a hospital run-down programme with beds elsewhere – instead of adopting a more radical approach and switching funds to domiciliary services. Further difficulties were encountered in an authority where social services were busy producing a decentralised structure while the housing department were busy centralising theirs, undermining the links forged between the two agencies. In another authority, where agencies were working towards joint schemes, difficulties were encountered with different conditions of service between staff from health and social services.

126. In addition, planning arrangements are very different. Health authorities have been planning services ten years ahead for some time now. Local authorities have a much shorter planning horizon because of the way they are funded, and the possibility of political change. One comment received was that 'local authorities don't joint plan because they don't plan at all'. However, comments were also received that health authority plans are sometimes little more than a loosely connected series of bids for resources from internal departments. Joint planning is more likely to progress where it builds on existing planning traditions.

127. In immediate practical terms the incentives for health and local authorities to co-operate are limited. Developing new services is hard work – especially if the main beneficiary is perceived to be some other agency. On the other hand, particularly at times of economic restraint and retrenchment, managers are not penalised for failing to develop services. Rather they are congratulated for keeping costs down. The main incentives are provided by job satisfaction following effective progress – very important for many of the staff met during the study. However, in some authorities there appeared to be a failure to recognise that under the White Paper proposals they are expected by government to increase their role in caring for both mentally handicapped and mentally ill people. Consequently there was a genuine lack of urgency, and lack of a willingness to extend their role and take the initiative. It is always easier to do nothing; and without adequate incentives and encouragement, the sheer inertia of the present arrangements appeared to dominate in some authorities.

128. The result of the general lack of incentive to co-operate and the contrasting management styles within health and local authorities is an

unduly rigid approach to problems. Community care in action often requires considerable flexibility – both at the operational and at the service planning levels. At the operational level, circumstances often change from day to day, especially where care is being provided to frail or sick people. In a hospital, there is no difficulty in adjusting the level of care, since the ward staff simply switch their attention to the individual requiring the additional services (provided of course that the hospital is adequately resourced in the first place). In the community, such adjustment requires a re-programming of schedules, often between agencies. Significant logistical problems can result. Where inter-agency communication is poor, there may not be sufficient flexibility to respond. As a result either the community placement breaks down, or services have to be provided at an unnecessarily high level all the time, with consequent waste and diseconomy. Integration of operational planning (assessment and prescription of services) is more difficult and less flexible under fragmented organisational arrangements.

129. At the service planning level, flexibility is also required as service developments are proceeding so rapidly. In one authority a purpose-built facility three years old was being abandoned (and converted for other uses) because rapid developments had rendered it obsolete. A policy of 'buy and convert' rather than purpose-build can often be more effective because of the shorter lead time required, and ability to sell when the property is no longer required. Cumbersome joint-planning arrangements do not appear to be sufficiently flexible to accommodate rapidly developing services.

*　　*　　*

130. The differences in incentive and style have resulted in an atmosphere where there are hard negotiations and 'horse trading' between separate, self contained and often fiercely independent organisations rather than joint planning and sharing of resources between partners seeking to serve the same clients more effectively. In short, bureaucracy rules. The latest DHSS circular still does not recognise this situation and prescribes more of the same – a strengthening of existing arrangements. The situation has been well summarised by Webb and Wistow (ref. 26):

'What was missing was evidence of any systematic understanding of the conditions which would have to be fulfilled if local actors were to carry out such processes (i.e. joint-planning). Those conditions may be briefly stated as the existence of a systems-wide perception of needs and service inter-dependencies; a developed analytical capacity; consensus on the nature of need and the care paradigms for meeting it; and the presence of organisational and professional altruism – a willingness to surrender resources and authority in order to achieve a systems-wide objective. These are highly demanding conditions. Indeed they imply patterns of inter-organisational and inter-professional behaviour quite different from those found in empirical studies of organisations. The picture which emerges in the literature suggests that: decision-making is typically incremental rather than rational and its focus parochial rather than systems-wide; organisations are primarily motivated by the maximisation, or defence, of sectional interests rather than the altruistic pursuit of common goals; and conflict, competition or the avoidance of interaction are more likely than consensus and the high levels of interaction implied by the joint planning model.'

INADEQUATE STAFFING ARRANGEMENTS

131. Staff are the key resource for community care. Appropriate buildings provide a suitable environment – for example, well designed day centres or correctly adapted housing. But it is people who do the caring. Sound

manpower planning and effective training are thus essential. Unfortunately, both appear conspicuous by their absence so far as community care is concerned.

132. Training is particularly important. People working in the community require a rather different approach from those working in a large hospital, although there is considerable overlap of basic skills. Community-based staff must be capable of working on their own, and be able to make decisions and adjust their patterns of working to fit in with the fluctuating needs of the people they serve, without immediate recourse to supervisors or more experienced colleagues. The work calls for greater flexibility, greater all round skills, use of judgement and ability to adapt. The person concerned must be able to liaise effectively with other workers helping the client; but generally the person who works in the community is on his or her own.

133. Table 22 below shows the way some of the major staff groups have been changing over the last ten years.

Table 22: STAFFING TRENDS, 1974–84
England only. Whole-time equivalents

	1974	1979	1984	% increase 1974–1984
Local Authority Staff				
Residential Care for Adults	48,800	56,800	64,200	32%
Adult Training Centre/Day Centre	8,100	11,400	15,000	87
Home Help Service	42,400	46,700	53,100	25
Other Support	1,400	1,600	2,200	63
OT's included above	N/A	N/A	900	N/A
Social Workers	17,000	22,700	24,300	43
NHS Staff				
Mental Illness Hospital Nurses	43,000	50,300	57,600	34
of which CPN's	N/A	1,100	2,200	N/A
Mental Handicap Hospital Nurses	21,000	25,800	30,000	43
Community Nurses	10,800	13,700	15,200	40

The training problem needs to be looked at both from the hospital and community care perspectives.

The hospital perspective

134. There has been a rapid increase in the number of nurses in mental handicap and psychiatric hospitals. Overall, over a third of the increase in NHS staff over the last ten years has occurred in these hospitals, at a time of declining patient numbers as Exhibit 15 shows. Mental handicap and

Exhibit 15

CHANGES IN HOSPITAL STAFF AND PATIENT NUMBERS IN ENGLAND, 1974-85

Index: 1974 = 100

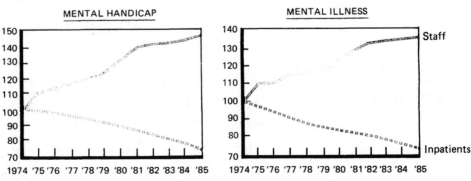

Source: Health and Personal Social Services Statistics for England 1986 Edition

psychiatric hospitals have long been inadequately staffed, and some redress has long been required. Furthermore, a resettlement programme no doubt needs additional staff to train participants in daily living skills etc; and an ageing more dependent residual population requires more care. It is nonetheless ironic that at a time when such hospitals are being run-down, such large increases in staff have occurred.

135. As a result, hospitals for mentally ill and mentally handicapped people are costing considerably more to run than they were a decade ago; and they are using money that could otherwise be used for bridging finance. A more effective strategy to improve the standard of service to clients might have involved the deployment of the extra staff in the community, accelerating the development of community care and the rundown of long-stay hospital provision.

136. At the same time, the future is not clear to most of the 70,000 people now working in large mental hospitals who will be displaced by their closure. Their skills, experience and dedication will go to waste, unless steps are taken to retrain them for work in the community. Suitable community placements and alternatives should be identified for these people who have the skills and experience of working with mentally handicapped and mentally ill people. Some may not be able to cope with the changes and challenges involved with the introduction of community care; but given suitable training, many would be ideal. At present very little is being done, and it is hardly surprising that many staff are apprehensive about their personal positions and thus less likely to support new initiatives.

137. There are some notable exceptions. In Exeter Health Authority the General Manager gave all his staff a no-redundancy guarantee, and subsequently found placements for all of them. As a result he has been one of the very first to close a large mental handicap hospital. However, where long-stay hospitals serve more than one authority and thus have more staff than can readily be absorbed in the community by one authority, it is difficult to give such a guarantee and remain within cost limits. At the national level, the National Health Service Training Authority (NHSTA) in collaboration with the Department of Education and Science, is planning to introduce a Health 'PICKUP' (professional, industrial and commercial updating) scheme (ref. 27) which will provide new learning and updating opportunities for people already working in nine key professions within the NHS. The new training will be in modular form, with each unit free standing; individuals may take a series of units, combining them to gain additional qualifications. A needs analysis is under way which will be completed by 1986, leading to the design and introduction of modules in 1987. In broad terms these fall into five areas:

- Clinical skills specific to the different professions
- Management skills, including the use of information technology
- Inter-personal skills with the patient and with other professions
- Communication skills to ensure an efficient and effective service and effective communication
- Teamwork skills.

Within this framework modules to help staff transfer from hospital to community could be designed. However, the NHSTA has only limited resources. And it is by no means certain that the needs of staff in the long-stay hospitals will receive priority.

The community perspective

138. There has also been a failure to provide the staff who will be required in the community in the future. The number of community psychiatric nurses in 1985 was less than 2,700. The severe shortage of domiciliary occupational

62

therapists (OTs) has also been a major and widely recognised problem for many years.

139. The skills of occupational therapists are in many ways central to the implementation of community care, in that OTs are currently responsible for the specification of activities for people to help them reach their maximum level of function and independence in all aspects of daily life, the assessment of handicap, and the selection of aids and design of adaptations to buildings. These skills should be at the forefront of an 'enabling' service. And yet the number of domiciliary OTs remains pitifully small. The latest figures from the DHSS (ref. 28) indicate that there are less than 1,000 whole-time equivalent posts in local authorities. This gives a ratio of less than 1:1,000 people in the community currently receiving some form of care. Many local authorities do not employ OTs at all; and in those that do, the OTs carry enormous caseloads – often limiting their work to the provision of aids which is only a part of their potential contribution. Given the growth in day care and in the number of very elderly people and the move to community care this situation is likely to worsen.

140. The DHSS has found that 'with growing demand for occupational therapy, there is a national shortage – creating difficulties in filling funded posts as well as limiting developments in the service' (ref. 29). However, the potential for an order-of-magnitude increase in OT numbers appears to be limited with the professional training schools working to capacity. More married women OTs are returning to work, giving a growth rate in number of 6% each year in the NHS over the last eight years, and numbers have further been enhanced by the employment of aides and technicians.

141. Potential for further expansion of occupational therapy numbers in the short-term is thus apparently limited. The training period for occupational therapists is a minimum of three years, to which must be added a further period in which to provide additional places in training schools. Recently the DHSS has announced plans for the establishment of a new school of occupational therapy at Christ Church College, Canterbury, to provide an additional 30 places a year from 1987 onwards. The possibility of establishing a second new school in the next two to three years in being actively explored. These developments, welcome though they are, are unlikely to result in any significant increase in the numbers of fully-trained practising occupational therapists for several years.

142. The OT problem illustrates the risks and difficulties inherent in a manpower planning approach which involves predicting the numbers required in each separate professional group and then attempting to deliver just the right mix. The skills described above for OTs are too important and too fundamental to the new community care service to be restricted to a small specialist cadre that cannot hope to meet demand in the foreseeable future. Some way of making these skills more widely available is needed, freeing the specialist OTs for specialist tasks that only they can do.

143. The concept of a 'core' of community care skills could be developed for all those involved in community-based care based on shared training. At present most staff providing care in the community were either trained and/or gained their experience in a different type of work:

- Both OTs and nurses are trained in hospital settings, although more recently community care is becoming an increasingly important element of their training
- Many home helps gained their experience providing a domestic service rather than a home care service
- Furthermore, each type of worker receives a different sort of training.

144. The nursing profession is beginning to tackle this issue with the recent

launch of 'Project 2000' by the United Kingdom Central Council (UKCC) for nursing, midwifery and health visiting (ref. 30). This project recognises that training should be more flexible and should include much more time in the community as part of the common foundation programme. At present these proposals are for the nursing profession. But there could be considerable advantages (including improved value for money) in sharing some elements of basic training with other professional groups. The occupational therapy profession has the basis of modular training in existence. Thus there is a 'helpers' course which takes 200 hours of training. There is then a conversion course for helpers based on in-service training over four years; and a conversion course from a similar profession such as nursing or physio-therapy. Both of these courses lead to qualification in occupational therapy. The three-year diploma course is the main form of training, however.

145. But, as is so often the case, the problem is not knowing in general terms what needs to be done, but rather securing action at the national level. As long ago as 1972, the Briggs Committee recommended that 'a new caring profession for the mentally handicapped should emerge gradually'. In 1975 the Jay Committee was set up to review this recommendation; and in their report published in 1979 (ref. 31) recommended a new training based on the certificate in social services, augmented by more specialist input on mental handicap. The Committee recognised that 'if this new qualifying training is to work smoothly and effectively the General Nursing Councils (GNCs) and Central Council for Education and Training in Social Work (CCETSW) will have to work in harmony and co-operation'.

146. The hoped-for harmony and co-operation did not materialise. So the then Secretary of State invited the GNCs and CCETSW to set up a joint group to review options for collaboration in training. A joint report was produced in 1983 (ref. 32) which recommended to the Council that 'they declare their support in principle for the development of shared training'. However progress towards this ideal has been slow. In one area visited, agreement was reached locally in 1984 on a joint course; but the course has not been validated by the English National Board and CCETSW even after prolonged discussions. Furthermore, CCETSW has now indicated that resolution of this problem is unlikely before 1990 at the earliest. If the principle of shared training proves so difficult for staff working with mentally handicapped people, then there is little chance of worthwhile progress being made with other groups of workers.

147. In summary, community care requires a new impetus in training and a different approach to manpower planning if the needs of existing hospital staff on the one hand and the needs for properly trained community care staff on the other are to be met. At present there seems to be small likelihood of the impetus occurring. As a result, the opportunities for improving care for people in the community are being put at risk.

*　　*　　*

148. Together, the problems described in this chapter constitute a formidable barrier to be overcome; and they have caused the slow and uneven progress towards community care that in turn is resulting in waste, inefficiency and less effective care than should be available to many people. As is almost always the case where local government is concerned, successful local initiatives – usually undertaken in spite of the nationally derived control systems, not because of them – point a possible way forward. Such initiatives form the subject of the next chapter of this report.

3. Radical Changes Needed

149. The previous two chapters paint a fairly bleak picture. Progress with community care is slow and uneven; and there are many obstacles in the way to ensure that this state of affairs continues. However, in practice the picture is not uniformly dark. There are many good community care schemes developing – in spite of the system rather than because of it. Many people are working hard to thread a way through the organisational maze and to overcome the financial obstacles because they believe that community care is the best way forward for their clients. But it is clear that more than fine tuning of the existing arrangements will be needed to make community care a local reality throughout England and Wales. The Commission has concluded that radical changes need urgent consideration, for the following reasons:

   (i) The success of some current local schemes shows that community-based care can bring great benefits to the quality of life for literally millions of people.

   (ii) But successful local schemes have only been possible because local people have, in effect, ignored the existing rules and taken radical action.

   (iii) Some apparently attractive strategic options have not received thorough evaluation.

Each of these reasons is discussed in more detail below.

POTENTIAL BENEFITS FROM COMMUNITY CARE: LESSONS FROM SUCCESSFUL SCHEMES

150. Quite apart from value for money considerations, the scale of the benefits that could follow from successful introduction of community-based care for frail elderly, mentally ill, physically handicapped, and mentally handicapped people is immense. Not only will the quality of life for many of the 350,000 people now in residential accommodation of one sort or another be improved; but the strain on the millions of people who are caring for relatives with limited support from public services could be substantially reduced. That such a goal is feasible is demonstrated by experience in areas which have moved ahead with community-based initiatives despite all the problems described earlier. Some of the initiatives that have come to the attention of the Commission's study team are described below. For reasons of space, only one (or at most two) schemes are referred to for each of the main groups of clients; the mentally handicapped, the mentally ill, the elderly mentally infirm, the frail elderly and the physically disabled as well as one example of a scheme for 'caring for the carers'. The Commission is not in any way suggesting that these examples represent an exhaustive list of successful community care initiatives. But what the examples do demonstrate is that community-based care need not be just another attractive concept.

Services for Mentally Handicapped People

151. In *Plymouth*, a strategic plan has been developed by an inter-authority planning initiative which has involved officers and members from Plymouth Housing Department, Devon County Council Social Services and Education Departments, and Plymouth Health Authority. The area had no large mental handicap hospital; but 144 people from the area were expected to be discharged from Starcross Hospital in Exeter Health Authority.

152. The plan envisages the accommodation of the people returning from hospital primarily into 30 houses with resident staff in support (staffed group homes) with a few of the more able in unstaffed group homes, plus a modest expansion to the number of residential home places. In support there is a health authority 'treatment unit' of 20 beds, and a social services short-stay facility of 24 beds. In addition, the plan contains proposals for a rationalisation and expansion of day care to provide a place for all the mentally handicapped people in Plymouth primarily in social education centres and a community day care programme.

153. Exhibit 16 shows the 1983 provision and the five-year target.

Exhibit 16

SERVICES FOR MENTALLY HANDICAPPED PEOPLE

Example: Plymouth serving 325,000

	1983 SITUATION	FIVE-YEAR TARGET
RESIDENTIAL SETTINGS		
Own home with external support only	4	30
Own home with resident support	–	130
With parents/guardians	300	300
Social Services residential home		
— In Plymouth	187	230
— Outside Plymouth	20	–
NHS Residential		
— In Plymouth	15	–
— Outside Plymouth	144	–
Short-term care/treatment		
— NHS	25	20
— Social Services	–	24
TOTAL PLACES	**695**	**734**
DAY FACILITIES		
NHS		
— Day care	40	–
— Work unit	30	30
Social Services		
— Adult Training Centres	305	–
— Social Education Centres	–	405
— Special Care Facilities	20	45
Voluntary Sector	55	62
Community Day Care ('on location')	–	180
TOTAL PLACES	**450**	**722**

Source: Strategic Plan for Services in Plymouth

The total cost to the NHS and social services departments is £3 million (at March 1984 prices). There is an additional cost to Supplementary Benefits of £600,000. The overall cost of the service is comparable to the cost of the previous hospital-based service. The balance of care is shifted dramatically more in favour of the community than was envisaged in the 1971 White Paper; so is cost, with 66% of the local expenditure on care of the mentally handicapped people being met from the social services' budget.

Table 23: COST OF SERVICES FOR MENTALLY HANDICAPPED PEOPLE IN PLYMOUTH
Annual Cost in £000s

	1983		1988 (Target)	
NHS	£2,120	71%	972*	34
Social Services	869	29	1868	66

* All at March 1984 prices

154. The Plymouth model is by no means unique. A similar pattern is being introduced in two of the other authorities visited. The North Western RHA is basing its strategy on small units of accommodation as outlined in its paper *A Model District Service* (ref. 33). A recent innovation in *South Glamorgan* takes the concept of community living to the point where individual mentally handicapped people are supported in their own homes through a 'Flexicare' scheme. Instead of using staff attached to specific group homes on a roster basis, this scheme uses a pool of community support staff who work flexible hours as needed. By allocating staff times precisely to the needs of residents, costs are kept down, and a more independent style of living is possible for clients within existing budgets. This type of 'care attendant' scheme has potential for the other priority groups as well. It could well form one of the main community care services in the future.

Services for Mentally Ill People

155. In *Torbay* a joint plan for service for mentally ill people has been produced. Here, the service is being built around community mental health centres, which act as the base for a team of mental health professionals and the focus for mental health services in the district. Residential accommodation is provided in the variety of settings shown in Exhibit 17, including a

Exhibit 17

SERVICES FOR MENTALLY ILL PEOPLE: RESIDENTIAL SETTINGS

Example: Torbay serving 225,000

PROVIDING AGENCY	FORM OF CARE	SERVICE
District housing Private sector	Unstaffed group homes with support	25 ordinary houses supported by domiciliary and day care provision
Voluntary sector	Voluntary sector group homes	4 group homes run by MIND
District housing Social Services Private sector	Sheltered lodgings	Normal housing with landladies or 'adult fostering'
District housing Housing association	Core and cluster scheme	3 or 4 houses supported by warden/general manager and domiciliary services
District housing Private housing Health and social services staff	Staffed group homes	4 houses for 4 or 5 people each with residential staff support
Private sector	Residential homes	Mainly for the older age range
Health authority	Health service hostels	3 hostels
Health authority	Hospital	60 beds (acute short-term)

Source: Mental Illness: A Strategy for the Future
(South Devon Social Services, Devon County Council)

number of in-patient beds (0.3 per 1,000 population which is at the bottom of the range proposed by the DHSS). Analysis of the costs of the service shows that a service can be provided within current financial provisions. Again the balance of care and expenditure is shifted dramatically more in favour of the community than was envisaged in the 1975 White Paper – 44% of expenditure planned for community care, as opposed to hospital or residential care.

156. The plan was produced locally, through close co-operation between those involved (a 'bottom up' approach to planning). As a result staff are committed to the plan. A further feature is the commitment to avoid professional demarcation and fragmentation as evidenced by the following extract from the plan:

'Each centre would build up a team of professional staff to meet its needs. For work in the community mental health centres, the particular professional training required is coming to be seen as of less importance than the aptitude for a new style of work.

It would be expected that the professional would embrace a truly multi-disciplinary style of working with little emphasis on hierarchy within the centre. This would imply acceptance of equal responsibility with others for the management and development of the centre.

Although members of staff would be drawn from a wide range of professional orientations e.g. social worker, doctor, nurse, psychologist, in practice professional role differentation would become of secondary importance. Primarily each team member will be seen as a 'mental health professional'. Given such a title, team members will find it possible to integrate separate skills into a realistic approach, so that as Professor Kathleen Jones suggests (ref. 34) there is 'no need to stand on professional dignity, they get on with the job'.

Services for Elderly People

157. In *Hastings*, initiatives to improve services for elderly mentally infirm people started from a realisation by the East Sussex Social Services Department that it had surplus residential accommodation in two homes, one of which was unsatisfactory; while a psycho-geriatrician in the Hastings Health Authority had simultaneously concluded that the long stay beds in a local hospital were unsatisfactory and too expensive. Consequently local NHS and social services staff worked out a service based on closure of the hospital beds; conversion of the newer home to accommodate elderly mentally infirm people, with upgraded facilities; conversion of the older home to provide day places for the Health District; transfer of funds from the hospital to pay for the new development (this freeing existing social services funds to provide a range of additional services in the community). Decisions about admission and discharge to the social services beds are made by the NHS psycho-geriatrician.

158. This example illustrates a number of points. As in Plymouth and Torbay, planning was initiated locally, so that local staff from different professional groups are committed to the scheme. An evolutionary approach was adopted, with initial difficulties turned to advantage and opportunities grasped to develop an integrated service. Many new initiatives are springing up in a 'chain reaction' following the early developments, by redeploying the savings that have been made – such as the appointment of community care staff and additional social work staff who will be adopting a more preventative approach. These initiatives were in turn made possible by the high degree of delegation and autonomy given to local staff and the release of funds that could be recycled.

159. In *Hillingdon* a different approach is bearing fruit. A comprehensive review of social services and housing for the elderly has been undertaken by

Hillingdon Borough Council in conjunction with the Hillingdon Health Authority. A 'balance of care' approach was adopted; this was originally devised within the DHSS, and subsequently developed in several counties in conjunction with the management consultants Arthur Anderson Ltd. Under this review, a team of professionals from a variety of backgrounds reassessed the existing recipients of care and identified the services most appropriate for them (irrespective of which services they were receiving at the time). The ensuing theoretical pattern of services was then compared with the existing pattern. It was evident that many people needed services that they could not obtain; while at the same time, other people received services that they did not need. In particular hospital beds were often occupied by people who no longer required treatment; while at the same time people elsewhere were unable to gain access. Moreover, homes for the elderly were often occupied by people who could cope in the community given appropriate support, and would be better placed there. And domiciliary services were not matching needs appropriately.

160. Following the review, a series of improvements were proposed. Homes for the elderly will accommodate more dependent people; the growth of neighbourhood and voluntary care will be promoted; home care and auxiliary nursing services will be combined and expanded. Overall, there is to be a major shift in the way services are used, leading to a mix of services better matched to people's needs.

Services for Younger Physically Handicapped People

161. In *Wigan*, the Fourways Day Centre provides multi-disciplinary help for young disabled people in the initial years after they have left school – a critical period. It involves the joint participation of Wigan Borough Council, NHS and Education departments and additional liaison with Employment Services, the Housing Department and voluntary organisations. The aims of the centre are to assess an individual's potential for future independent living, employment, further education or vocational training and to seek out resources in the community which enable young people to maintain the level of functioning achieved during their two year (maximum) stay at the unit. This period at the unit has been described as 'transitional rehabilitation'. The unit is an example of a 'resource centre' which acts as a focus for joint working. Several authorities had joint schemes for promoting accommodation for disabled people. One such example was being provided in Hereford with staff from the NHS, Social Services and Housing Departments working together.

162. There are examples of severely disabled people living in the community (ref. 35). One of the best is provided by the *Centre for Independent Living* based at Lee Court Cheshire Home in Hampshire (ref. 36). Housing is provided which is appropriately adapted (some bought by parents). The Social Services Department and Health Authority have contributed funds to a trust for purchasing care which is administered by the Leonard Cheshire Foundation. The disabled person buys in the help needed with this money, topped up by his or her own social security benefits. Thus the disabled people construct their own packages of care and employ their own staff in a highly autonomous fashion. They effectively do their own 'joint-planning'.

RADICAL ACTION NECESSARY

163. Each of the schemes described above demonstrates different features of community care. Indeed, the sheer variety of initiatives is one of the notable features of current developments ('a hundred flowers bloom', as Sir Kenneth Stowe, First Permanent Secretary of DHSS, described the current situation to a recent meeting of the House of Commons Select Committee on Social Services). However, one lesson is clear. In their different ways, all the

69

successful schemes known to the Commission involve a radical departure from the generally accepted ways of doing things. Specifically, all the schemes are characterised by:

   (i) *Strong and committed local 'champions' of change.* Probably the single most important factor common to all the successful community care initiatives observed during the study was the presence of people with vision, determination and stamina who had pushed developments along. It was always possible to trace initiatives back to one or two people who would not take no for an answer. Where a strong able social services director (and/or divisional director) is opposite an equally able and determined NHS general manager mutual trust can develop with both sides working hard to avoid situations that might undermine this trust. This relationship appeared to be far more important than joint planning machinery – although interestingly, the joint planning machinery also seemed to work better under strong direction.

  (ii) *Focus on action, not bureaucratic machinery.* The most successful part of the current joint planning machinery appears to be the sub-committees appointed to plan services for individual client groups where these sub-committees are given precise terms of reference to achieve a particular task. This task may be to co-ordinate arrangements for the closure of a hospital; or to plan a new pattern of services in the community. By setting up a multi-disciplinary, multi-agency team together to *focus on a particular topic*, the difficulties of joint planning outlined in chapter 2 seem to be reduced, and coherent plans emerge. However, they take considerable amounts of time, effort and energy; and authorities must be prepared to invest heavily if results are to be forthcoming. The secret appears to be to focus the work of such teams under strong chairmanship within agreed time-scales, and with precise terms of reference and budgets.

 (iii) *Locally-integrated services.* Many of the characteristics described in the previous paragraphs come together in services that are integrated at a local level. A number of successful variations about this theme were observed including some of the examples already quoted. They have in common the 'linking' of services and agencies locally. For convenience the report uses the acronym 'LINCC' schemes to describe them (locally integrated community care schemes). Some of the common features of such schemes are:

    – A significant degree of delegated authority within both NHS and social services, with agencies' management structures matched so that managers from both (or all) 'sides' can relate to each other on a one-to-one basis. In East Sussex, for instance, local social services managers are given a budget (establishing a local 'cost centre') which relates to a number of existing resources; they are then allowed to change the use of their resources locally within this budget. New ways of accounting are being introduced which put an emphasis on controlling outputs rather than inputs. This means controlling and monitoring what is happening to people, ensuring that needs and services match – in contrast to the more usual input-based expenditure budgets for individual services

    – Services are provided to a 'local' area that is sufficiently small and self contained for it to have a recognisable identity, and for professionals to know each other on a personal basis. Again, experience in East Sussex is showing that the more flexible method of working and the more immediate response that has become possible are building links locally between East Sussex Social Services and the NHS (including GPs and community nurses). Thus, in Brighton a scheme for community care of mentally handicapped people benefits from a matching of the area of responsibility of the social services manager and the unit general manager for mental health services. There are now plans to align the responsibilities of individual social services field work managers with those of neighbourhood nurse managers to integrate their activities still further

— Strategic and operational planning is linked; staff responsible for service planning are either the same, or are in close touch with staff responsible for operation planning. For example, in Plymouth, a Housing Project Group includes a representative from Plymouth Housing Department, an administrator from Plymouth Health Authority, the hospital social worker who had personally assessed all the people to be discharged into the community, and a joint co-ordinator appointed by the Health Authority (using joint finance) to work in the Social Services Department. This group establishes houses for mentally handicapped people, matching the houses to the people, taking account of individuals' disabilities and of friendships.

In some situations, service integration is promoted by one authority taking the lead. In one health authority visited the unit general manager for mental handicapped services controlled both hospital and community services. Because of this, the run-down and potential closure of the hospital was a positive challenge rather than a threat – since her job was independent of the mode of care. Also she was able to manage the transfer in a planned integrated way, with the phased cash flow totally under her control and with the ability to guarantee jobs to the staff in the hospital. As a result plans were clear, and progress was on target – but with very little contribution from the social services department. In several authorities visited plans were well advanced to transfer all mental handicap services across to the social services department – as first proposed by the Jay Committee and subsequently endorsed by the House of Commons Select Committee. In all of these authorities mutual trust and respect were high, allowing the health authorities to transfer services and resources without too many qualms.

(iv) *Focus on the local neighbourhood.* By definition, community care involves looking after people, if not in their own homes, in the communities and neighbourhoods where they and their families have lived. The Barclay Report (ref. 37) recommended 'community social work' as the way forward. And neighbourhood nursing has recently been proposed in the Cumberlege Report (ref. 38). The Government has also indicated that it regards the co-ordination and mobilisation of voluntary resources to be an important element of community care; and this, too, requires close links with communities. In Exeter Health Authority, there is a process known as 'locality planning', with six local planning groups involving local professionals as well as interested members of the community (such as parents of mentally handicapped people). The local planning groups identify needs for community-based care in their own patches, and develop plans which are then submitted to a central development group. The development group then sorts these plans and tries to find resources to match the priorities.

(v)   *Team approach*. The Court Report (ref. 40) introduced the idea of community handicap teams; and the National Development Team has developed the idea for mentally handicapped people in the form of community mental handicap teams (CMHTs). These teams combine the work of psychiatrists, psychologists, social workers, community psychiatric nurses (CPNs) and occupational therapists. The social worker and CPN tend to be full-time, with the other professionals available on a sessional basis. Resource centres are also useful. These are often former residential homes or day centres which play several roles at once including long and short stay home, day centre (possibly offering both rehabilitation and 'drop-in' facilities), crisis centre, base for community staff, contact point, focus for services. Usually such resource centres involve staff from both health and social services:

- The 'community units' proposed by the National Development Team for Mentally Handicapped People can operate in this way and one such centre visited during the study is acting as both a focus and a 'launch point' for community-based services
- In Sheffield, Elderly Persons Support Units (EPSUs) provide day care and a base for home care staff for specific neighbourhoods
- Many primary care teams have a range of services under one roof. For instance in one health centre visited there are general practitioners, dentists, health visitors and community nurses (some in the treatment room), community psychiatric nurses, health authority-employed speech therapist, sex therapist, dietician and community physiotherapist, a local authority social worker, voluntary workers doing counselling provided by the Marriage Guidance Council and someone giving social security advice.

(vi)   *Partnership between statutory services and voluntary organisations*. Some of the most cost-effective and flexible services encountered during the study were provided by voluntary organisations, such as *Home Start* and the *Crossroads* care attendant schemes for helping to support the caring relatives of elderly and disabled people. Quite apart from emotional and financial costs that carers now incur, the scheme results in a considerable saving of public funds. For example, in a recent study of *Crossroads* schemes in Essex (ref. 39) the following conclusions were drawn:

- Two-thirds of the disabled people supported in the schemes are so severely handicapped that they can be left for no more than an hour; they need help with basic personal care, toileting and also regularly need help at night. Clearly this group could not expect to live independently in the community without a carer
- Most of the disabled people have one main carer who lives with them. That carer shoulders the brunt of the responsibility for care. Apart from *Crossroads* the carers do so with no real prospect of sharing the burden
- All the joint assessors used in the study felt that in the majority of cases *Crossroads* was providing the kind of help that the family required. This conclusion was re-inforced by their judgement that a care attendant scheme would have to be re-invented if *Crossroads* lapsed. If the level of service was to be maintained, the alternative statutory services required would cost approximately twice the annual grant to the *Crossroads* schemes
- Given a positive message of support coupled with regular short periods of relief and confidence in the care attendants, the

majority of disabled people and carers alike see *Crossroads* as a long-term alternative to residential care.

164. It will be evident even for the most casual reader that the characteristics described above amount to a radical departure from the generally accepted ways of doing things at present in the NHS and within local government. To be specific:

- The public service is generally suspicious of personal leadership by officers. Members often feel threatened by it: Committee-based consensus is the norm, particularly in local authority social services departments. In most cases, champions of change are likely to be regarded as 'difficult' mavericks, to be controlled rather than encouraged

- It will be unkind even to discuss the concept that the existing bureaucracies within the public service should focus on action. They usually exist to ensure fairness, to prevent mistakes and to see that rules are followed. The training and instinct of most administrators in the NHS and local government is, entirely understandably, to play safe and avoid risks and to keep their political masters content. Unfortunately, the lack of community care does not appear to excite much political interest at the local level

- Particularly in local government, and within social services especially, members and senior officers are usually reluctant to see increased delegation of authority and responsibility to the operating level. Their priority is, again very understandably, to retain effective central control so as to prevent some tragedy that will attract unfavourable media attention

- Integration of local services runs directly counter to professional and bureaucratic pressures, not to mention the current financial framework. The NHS manager advocating 'handing over' part of the service to local government would be taking a serious risk with his or her career. Of course the same would apply within local government

- The inter-professional tensions e.g. between medicine and nursing, hospital and community-based care, home helps, occupational therapists and health visitors, social services and housing, are very great, especially at a time of change and uncertainty as at present

- Almost invariably, the local neighbourhood will be very much smaller than the area defined by existing district and county boundaries – hence the preferred local authority housing 'patch' of 1,500 – 2,000 dwellings.

165. Indeed, in the light of these problems, it is little short of amazing that *any* successful community-based schemes have been introduced. What is clear is that it is simply unrealistic to rely on having the right people in the right place at the right time to overcome such formidable obstacles. Radical changes must therefore be considered.

STRATEGIC OPTIONS FOR CONSIDERATION

166. The objective of any changes should be to create an environment in which locally integrated community care can flourish. The present statutory framework constitutes a barrier to the necessary changes. The focus is on services, not clients; decisions about different services for the same client are taken in different agencies and may need to be referred upwards through different professional hierarchies. Centralised planning arrangements in a range of different agencies do not allow the necessary degree of flexibility and local delegation required for LINCC schemes to operate effectively.

And, of course, local authorities, NHS and social security policies and the pattern of distribution of finance are out of alignment.

167. The management focus should be on local operations rather than (as at present) on the headquarters organisation and joint planning machinery. A housing authority may have difficulty in relating to a health authority or a personal social services department for all the reasons outlined; but an individual housing manager can (and often does) relate readily to a GP or a social worker with whom he or she works discussing the needs of individual people on day-to-day basis either in the same building or close by.

168. Finance presents a more fundamental problem, however. Realigning financial responsibilities in order to provide the right environment for LINCC schemes requires some adjustment to the organisational framework for community care. The analysis in chapter 2 of the inter-agency relationships concluded that the current arrangements with separately funded agencies requesting services from each other are unsatisfactory. A more rational way of arranging services would be for one agency to take lead responsibility (and with it both control of the budget and accountability for its appropriate use) and to 'buy in' services as necessary from other agencies.

169. The DHSS has in effect already introduced ways of changing the relationship between health authorities and other agencies in a modest way by introducing joint finance, and more recently by introducing transfer payments. Under these arrangements, services can be provided by other agencies and funded by health authorities. While both of these developments have been useful, joint finance amounts to less than 1% of the total budgets of health authorities and is, in any case, restricted to a limited time-scale.

170. However, the provision of service is only one part of the process of care. The sequence of events when somebody requires care is:

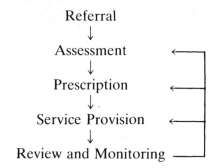

In practice some element of service provision can often be readily sub-contracted to other agencies: having responsibility for care does not inevitably mean that service delivery must be provided 'in-house'. However, under current arrangements, where community care is concerned there is little subcontracting of service provision. Even where services are provided by other agencies (e.g. private residential care) there is no contractual relationship between the agency responsible for care and the agency providing the service. Conversely, the care agencies cannot easily buy in other services (e.g. housing) which are an essential part of the package of care for their clients.

171. The staff responsible for assessment, prescription of packages of care and review are mainly employed either by NHS authorities or social services departments. Staff such as housing managers control access to particular services, but are less involved with assembling packages of care. This implies that health authorities and social services departments should form the central agencies controlling budgets and buying in services as necessary. However, having two separate services in the position of buying-in would only work if a sharp demarcation line could be drawn between them. As already outlined there is at present considerable confusion over the different

roles of the two agencies, with gaps and overlaps occurring. At the very least the demarcation line should be redefined. This has been suggested by a number of people – in particular the Association of County Councils in its recent publication *Strategies for Community Care* (ref. 40):

'The preferred solution, therefore, rather than specifically imposing or transferring duties to local authorities, lies in more clearly defining the responsibilities of the health service and the other services on the boundaries of the social services by legislation or by other government action.'

172. Other staff in authorities visited during the study have made the same point, requesting a clear division of responsibility between health and social services. However, there must be doubt as to whether this is feasible or desirable. Even if such a line could be defined the problems of how to allocate the budget would remain. A single budget and single manager for each care group would appear to be more straightforward; but the difficulty is how to achieve such an arrangement.

173. In the case of mental handicap services, the difficulties have been resolved in some authorities by the social services department taking over the whole service to become the 'lead' agency, although with the NHS retaining responsibility for a small number of the most severely handicapped people. A similar arrangement may be possible for physically handicapped people. This would not be so easy to achieve for the other client groups where there will always remain a significant health care component. For these groups some form of joint budget may be necessary, although for services for mentally ill people, the health service has such a predominant role that it may be preferable for the health service to take over the whole service in much the same way that some local authorities are taking over responsibility for services for mentally handicapped people.

174. Hence, while there are a number of possible strategic options for organising and funding community care, the Commission considers the following to be promising enough to warrant serious examination by an independent review:

(i) Local authorities should be made responsible for the long term care where required of **mentally and physically handicapped people in the community**; except for the most severely disabled who require medical supervision, and the resources necessary to do this should be identified and, where appropriate, transferred from the NHS.

(ii) For **care of elderly people in the community** a single budget in an area should be established by contributions from the NHS and local authorities the amount to be determined in each case by a formula agreed centrally. This budget should be under the control of a single manager who will purchase from whichever public or private agency he sees fit the appropriate services for elderly people in the community in the areas for which he is responsible. The manager's activities should be overseen by a small joint board of NHS and local authority representatives.

(iii) For **mentally ill people in the community,** the NHS will inevitably remain the prime authority responsible for care but nevertheless there remains an important role for social services. Two alternatives should be evaluated:

– Assigning to the NHS responsibility for all services; but that when it requires services from local authorities it should purchase these, with the local authority acting as the contractor

– An arrangement similar to that proposed above for services for elderly people.

In addition, for all client groups, care funded by Supplementary Benefits in the private or voluntary sector should be co-ordinated with care provided by the relevant local social services department or NHS authority.

175. Some preliminary work has already been undertaken on reviewing some of these issues in relation to residential care. In 1984 a joint central/local government working party was set up to examine the scope for improving collaboration between the DHSS and local authorities over financial support for residents of private and voluntary care homes (ref. 18). Both main recommendations have been accepted. Pilot studies are being set up to explore the feasibility of extending local authorities' existing multi-disciplinary assessment arrangements to anyone in residential care claiming benefit. The studies will also consider the feasibility of local authorities advising DHSS local offices on an appropriate level of payment for particular homes. In addition, a further central/local government working party has been set up to consider possible solutions to the problems created by the existing parallel system of local authority and Supplementary Benefit support for people in residential care.

176. Useful though the working parties will doubtless prove, more will be required. In parallel with possible changes in the organisational framework for community care, the present staff training and qualifying arrangements should be reviewed. One possible way forward could be to extend the concept of the common foundation programme proposed in Project 2000 to all professionals working in the community. A basic training would lead initially to a basic grade 'community care worker' who could act as a generalist and main contact for people in the community. This basic training would need to be recognised by the various professional bodies, and to give 'advanced standing' towards professional qualifications. Further specialist training (in occupational therapy, mental health, social work etc) could then be added, leading eventually to the various professional qualifications – in the same way that health visitors training is added on to an initial nursing qualification; and the in-service conversions course is added on to the initial occupational therapy 'helpers' course. Training undertaken in this way could then occur throughout a person's working life rather than just at the beginning. Extra modules could be undertaken as experience is gained, interests develop and needs in the community emerge. This sort of 'whole life' training has been proposed in the recent White Paper *Working Together – Education and Training* (ref. 42). Such specialists could be called in by community care workers as necessary. In this way better value for money and greater flexibility would be produced with a reduction in demarcation lines. Basic occupational therapy tasks (e.g. fitting simple aids) and nursing tasks (e.g. help with bathing) could be undertaken by people with basic training in community care rather than by fully trained professionals who take a long time and considerable expense to train, and who are only available in small numbers.

177. A high level review of these and other possibilities appears necessary. This report has shown that as background to the evaluation of the various strategic options, it will be essential to:
    (a) Examine how the transfer of resources from the NHS to local authorities can be speedily effected, matching the transfer of responsibility for particular client groups
    (b) Remove the financial disincentives to local authorities which deter them from playing their part in the move to community care
    (c) Identify how the operation of RAWP and GRE systems can be co-ordinated, so that funds are targeted to reflect the needs of different client groups and geographical areas
    (d) Find a financial means of ensuring adequate bridging for the change from residential to community care; while at the same time find ways

of increasing the rate of change to reduce the substantial amounts of bridging finance that will otherwise be necessary

(e) Determine how community care policies and Supplementary Benefit arrangements can be co-ordinated to remove the policy conflicts and perverse incentives that exist

(f) Identify a system that allows the proper care to be delivered to individual patients in the right place at the right cost (and price)

(g) Find a mechanism for co-ordinating manpower planning including re-deployment and training needs, so that large groups of people are not left either without a role or are inadequately trained for a new one

(h) Ensure that cost-effective voluntary organisations are not starved of funds for reasons unrelated to their potential contribution to the support of clients and those caring for them in the community.

*　　*　　*

The Commission will be glad to contribute to any such review that might be undertaken, in any way that is appropriate to its independence. What is not tenable is to do nothing about the present financial, organisational and staffing arrangements. This will have serious consequences. Progress towards community care will continue to be slow; and the uneven pattern of services will persist. The switch from hospitals to residential care funded through Supplementary Benefits will continue. The opportunity presented by the closure of large psychiatric and mental handicap hospitals and to build community services will pass. A pattern of care based on private residential care will become entrenched. In short, the care provided for some of the most deprived members of society will continue to be neither as economic, efficient nor as effective as it can or should be.

References

1. Harding T (1986) 'A Stake in Planning: Joint Planning and the Voluntary Sector' London, National Council for Voluntary Organisations

2. Department of Health and Social Security, Scottish Office, Welsh Office and Northern Ireland Office (1981). 'Growing Older' Cmnd 8173 London, HMSO

3. Willmott P (1986) 'Social Networks, Informal Care and Public Policy' London, Policy Studies Institute

4. Department of Health and Social Security (1981). 'Care in Action: A handbook of Policies and Priorities for the Health and Personal Social Services in England' London, HMSO

5. Department of Health and Social Security and Welsh Office (1971). 'Better Services for the Mentally Handicapped'. Cmnd 4683. London, HMSO

6. Department of Health and Social Security (1975). 'Better Services for the Mentally Ill' Cmnd 6233. London, HMSO

7. Social Services Committee, 1984/85 session (1985). 'Second Report. Community Care with Special Reference to Adult Mentally Ill and Mentally Handicapped People'. London, HMSO

8. Jones K (1985) 'After Hospital: a study of long-term psychiatric patients in York'. York Department of Social Policy and Social Work, University of York

9. Kay A and Legg C (1986) 'Discharged to the Community' A review of housing and support in London for people leaving psychiatric care'. London Housing Research Group City University

10. Audit Commission (1985). 'Managing Social Services for the Elderly More Effectively' London, HMSO

11. Gibbons J, Jennings C and Wing JK (1982) 'Psychiatric Care in Eight Register Areas in Great Britain 1976–81' Southampton Care Register, Knowle Hospital, Fareham, Hants

12. Ernst and Whinney (1986) 'Survey of Private and Voluntary Residential and Nursing Homes for the Department of Health and Social Security' London, Ernst and Whinney

13. Resource Allocation Working Party, Department of Health and Social Security (1976). 'Sharing Resources for Health in England' London, HMSO

14. Department of Health and Social Security (1983). 'Health Service Development: Care in the Community and Social Finance' Circular HC (83) 6/LAC(83)5. London, DHSS

15. Department of Health and Social Security (1981). 'Care in the Community: A Consultative Document on Moving Resources for Care in England' HC (81)9/LAC(81)5 London, DHSS

16. Audit Commission (1986). 'Managing the Crisis in Council Housing' London, HMSO

17. Audit Commission (1985). 'Capital Expenditure Controls in Local Government in England' London, HMSO

18. Joint Central and Local Working Party 1985 (1985) 'Supplementary Benefit and Residential Care' report London, DHSS

19. Association of Directors of Social Services (1985) 'Who goes Where: A profile of elderly people who have recently been admitted to residential homes', ADSS

20. Department of Health and Social Security (1986) 'Collaboration between the NHS, Local Government and Voluntary Organisations: Joint Planning and Collaboration' Draft Circular London, DHSS

21. Welsh Office (1983) 'All Wales Strategy for the Development of Service for Mentally Handicapped People'. Cardiff, Welsh Office

22. Welsh Office (1985) 'A Good Old Age: An Initiative on the Care of the Elderly in Wales' Cardiff, Welsh Office

23. Wistow G and Hardy B (1986) 'Transferring Care: Can Financial Incentive Work?' Health Care UK 1986 London, CIPFA

24. Woof K, Rose S and Street J 'Community Psychiatric Nursing Services in Salford, Southampton and Worcester' In Contributions to Health Service Planning and Research (Editor Wing J K) to be published, HMSO

25. Working Group on Joint Planning (1985) 'Progress in Partnership' London, DHSS

26. Wistow G and Webb A (1985) 'Studies in Central-Local Relations', London, Allen and Unwin

27. NHSTA and Department of Education and Science (1986) 'Creating a Framework for the Health Pick-up' London, NHSTA and DES

28. DHSS (1985) 'Occupational Therapy Service: National Health Service and Local Authority Social Services' Note. London, DHSS

29. DHSS (1985) 'Government Response to the Second Report from the Social Services Committee 1984–5 Session' Cmnd 9674 London, HMSO

30. United Kingdom Central Council for Nursing, Midwifery and Health Visiting (1986) 'Project 2000: A New Preparation for Practice' London, UKCC

31. Committee of Enquiry into Mental Handicap Nursing and Care (1979) Report Cmnd 7468–1 London, HMSO

32. Joint Working Group on Training for Staff Working with Mentally Handicapped People (1982) 'Co-operation in Training' London, Edinburgh, Belfast, General Nursing Councils/CCETSW

33. North Western Regional Health Authority (1982) 'Services for People who are Mentally Handicapped: A Model District Service' Manchester, NWRHA

34. Jones K (1979) 'Integration or Disintegration in Mental Health Services' University of York. Royal Society of Medicine (72)

35. Shearer A (1984) 'Living Independently' Kings Fund and Centre of Environment for the Handicapped. London, Kings Fund and CEH

36. Shearer A (April 1984) 'Independence is the Name of the Game' Voluntary Action Vol 2 No. 3 pages 10 – 11

37. National Institute of Social Work Working Party (1982) 'Social Workers: Their Role and Tasks' London, NCVO, NISW

38. Community Nursing Review DHSS (1986) 'Neighbourhood Nursing – A Focus for Care' London, HMSO

39. Committee on Child Health Services (1976) 'Fit for the Future' Cmnd 6684. London, HMSO

40. Cooper M (1985) 'Hard-Won Reality: An Evaluation of the Essex Crossroads Care Attendant Schemes', Essex County Council

41. Association of County Councils (1985) 'Strategies for Community Care' London, ACC

42. Department of Education and Science (1986) 'Working Together – Education and Training' Cmnd 9823 London, HMSO

43. Department of Health and Social Security (1980) 'Mental Handicap: Progress, Problems and Priorities' A Review of Mental Handicap Services in England since the 1971 White Paper 'Better Services for the Mentally Handicapped' London, DHSS

44. Wistow G (1985) 'Community Care for the Mentally Handicapped: Disappointing Progress.' Health Care UK 1985 London, CIPFA

45. National Health Service Health Advisory Service (1982) 'The Rising Tide: Developing Services for Mental Illness in Old Age' Sutton, NHSHAS

46. Richmond Fellowship Enquiry (1983) 'Mental Health and the Community' London, Richmond Fellowship Press

47. COHSE Working Party (1984) 'The Future of Psychiatric Services' London, Centurion Press

48. MIND (1983) 'Common Concern: MIND's Manifesto for a Comprehensive Mental Health Service'. London, MIND Publications.

49. Department of Health and Social Security (1977) 'Joint Care Planning: Health and Local Authorities' Circular HC (77) 17/LAC(77) 10 London, DHSS

50. Oglesby P R (1983) Report on the Review of Attendance Allowance and Mobility Allowance procedures and of medical adjudication. Unpublished, DHSS

Appendices

The following appendices are included with this report:

A – *Background to Government Community Care Policies.* This describes the evolution of national policy towards care for frail elderly, mentally ill, and mentally and physically handicapped people from the early 1970's onwards.

B – *Source and Derivation of Numerical Information.* This provides background information to the data presented in tables and exhibits contained in the main report.

C – *Social Security Benefits.* This attempts to describe the social security benefits that affect community care.

D – *Survey of Private and Voluntary Homes and Supplementary Benefit Expenditure.* This summarises the results of a survey carried out by the Commission in the course of the study. It also contains the Commission's estimate of the current level of expenditure on Supplementary Benefit payments for board and lodging to individuals in private and voluntary homes.

A – BACKGROUND TO GOVERNMENT COMMUNITY CARE POLICIES

1. The promotion of community care, and the reduction of institutional care is not a new phenomenon. In the case of services for mentally ill people, the present movement began in the 1930s, was interrupted by the war, and then really took off in the late 1950s. The peak bed occupancy of long-stay institutions was 1954. Since then it has been declining steadily with no particular acceleration recently. Much the same is true of mental handicap hospitals but the pace of change has been slower. Elderly and younger physically handicapped people have always been cared for primarily in the community although many of the most disabled people have been restricted to institutions in the past.

2. Thus, during 1981 the Government stated in a handbook of policies and priorities for the health and personal social services in England entitled *Care in Action* (ref. 4) that 'it has been a major policy objective for many years to foster and develop community care for the main client groups – elderly, mentally ill, mentally handicapped and disabled people and children – as well as for the special and smaller groups such as alcoholics'.

3. Within the same handbook particular emphasis was placed on services for these groups as follows:

'The Secretary of State expects authorities to give priority to the further development of services, both statutory and voluntary for the needs as locally assessed, of the following *priority groups:*

(a) *Elderly people, especially the most vulnerable and frail.* The number of people over 75 is increasing and those who need care have often been provided with unacceptably low standards of service, particularly in some aspects of long-term care

(b) *Mentally ill people.* This group is frequently provided with services of inadequate standard and services need developing in more accessible facilities

(c) *Mentally handicapped people.* This group is also often not provided with services of adequate standard and many services need development in more appropriate locations and on a different model

(d) *Physically and sensorily handicapped people.* Services to meet the needs of this group are frequently inadequate.'

GUIDELINES ON SERVICES FOR PRIORITY GROUPS

4. In 1970 care in the community for the fourth priority group of physically and sensorily handicapped people was strengthened by the Chronically Sick and Disabled Persons Act. In addition to *Care in Action*, three White Papers have been published setting out policies for the priority groups. In 1971 a White Paper entitled *Better Services for the Mentally Handicapped* (ref. 5) led the way, with a bold outline of a 20-year shift in provision from a hospital-based service to a community-based one. *Better Services for the Mentally Ill* (ref. 6) was published in 1975. This was followed in 1981 by a White Paper on services for elderly people entitled '*Growing Older*' (ref. 2).

Services for Mentally Handicapped People

5. *Better Services for the Mentally Handicapped* outlined the principles that should underpin community care services; and provided guidance to

local authorities and health authorities on the lines on which the Government wished their services to develop. The paper identified 'a serious shortage of adult training centres, gross shortage of residential accommodation, and great need for more trained staff of all kinds'. It also identified many shortfalls in the hospital service and as a result outlined a 20-year programme for switching services from the hospitals to the community as summarised in Table A – 1 (from Table 5 of the White Paper).

Table A – 1: SERVICES FOR MENTALLY HANDICAPPED ADULTS

	Places for Adults (age 16+)		
	Required		Provided
	Per 100,000 Total Population	Total England and Wales 1969	Total England and Wales 1969
Occupation and Training for Adults:			
In the Community—			
(i) for adults living in the community	130	63,700	24,500
(ii) for adults coming by day from hospital	20	9,800	100
In Hospitals—			
(iii) for in-patients	35	17,200	30,000*
(iv) for day patients	10	4,900	200*
Residential Care in the Community (including short-stay):			
(i) in local authority, voluntary or privately owned residential homes	60	29,400	4,300
(ii) foster homes, lodgings, etc.	15	7,400	550
Hospital Treatment:			
(i) for in-patients	55	27,000	52,100†
(ii) for day patients	10	4,900	500*

Source: Table 5. Better Services for the Mentally Handicapped
* Estimated
† NHS beds allocated to mental handicap

The switch required a significant expansion in social services provision since in August 1959 the Minister of Health by a direction under the *National Health Service Act* 1959 laid a duty on local authorities to provide a full range of community services for mentally handicapped people, including residential accommodation and day services. The guidelines in the White Paper have substantially been updated in 1985 in Annex 2 of the Government's Response to the Select Committee's Report (ref. 29).

6. Since the publication of the White Paper there has been a succession of reports charting progress, including for example the DHSS's own report *Mental Handicap: Progress, Problems and Priorities* (1980) (ref. 43) and more recently in 1985 *Community Care for the Mentally Handicapped: Disappointing Progress* by Gerald Wistow (ref. 44).

7. However, since 1971, there has been considerable development in concepts of care in the community. As early as 1974, it had become clear that the implementation of the White Paper was not taking place as planned. As a result of this, in February 1975, Mrs Barbara Castle, the then Secretary of State announced three new initiatives:

(i) The establishment of the National Development Group for mentally handicapped people.

(ii) The establishment of a Committee of Enquiry into mental handicap nursing and care under the chairmanship of Mrs Peggy Jay.

(iii) The intention to establish a Development Team to offer advice and assistance to health and local authorities in the planning and operation of their services to mentally handicapped people.

8. The National Development Group published a number of papers on various aspects of the care of mentally handicapped people, including five pamphlets on a variety of topics (including day care and planning) as well as checklists for monitoring and improving services. These reports have been seminal in the development of services. The National Development Team over the years has both charted progress and contributed to the thinking about the ways in which the White Paper proposals should be put into practice. In particular the team has proposed the introduction of community mental handicap teams, community units and has proposed a more precise role for residual hospital facilities. The Jay Committee's main recommendations concerned staffing and training arrangements, but also included proposals for a model of care based primarily on small units of accommodation. The Select Committee endorsed this view (recommendation 39): 'we recommend that new residential services for all but a small minority of mentally handicapped adults be in the form of ordinary housing within the wider community'.

9. The pattern of service development observed in practice involves a combination of these proposals, and also includes local variation and initiatives. Furthermore, in the most advanced authorities the concepts of community care have been pushed much further than was envisaged in the White Paper. This situation was noted in the DHSS's own review of mental handicap published in 1980 in paragraph 2.47 where it said 'we think it likely that the White Paper over-estimated the number of hospital places which will eventually be required'. In consequence, the targets have been revised in 1985 in Annex 2 of the Government's Response to the Select Committee Report (ref. 29) although:

'The total number of places including respite care places (although this can be provided in the family's own home by substitute families) provided by the NHS, local authorities and other bodies should probably be about the same as envisaged by the White Paper. Health and local authorities might therefore use figures on the total residential provisions (adding NHS and local authority targets together) envisaged in the White Paper (155 places per 100,000 population aged 16 and over) as a rough guide to the total residential provision needed for adults, bearing in mind that the level of family support available will, to some extent, influence the provision required'.

Services for Mentally Ill People

10. The 1975 White Paper, *Better Services for the Mentally Ill*, proposed a new model for mental health services and specified four broad policy objectives:

(i) The expansion of local authority personal social services to provide residential, domiciliary, day care and social work support.
(ii) The relocation of specialist services in local settings.
(iii) The establishment of the right organisational links.
(iv) A significant improvement in staffing.

As with mentally handicapped people, government guidelines were updated in an Annex to the Government's response to the Select Committee's Report (ref. 29, Annex 1).

11. At the centre of the new model of services to a district is the psychiatric unit, normally based at the district general hospital (DGH) although 'many mental illness hospitals have built up community elements and links which enable them to provide a 'DGH type of service'. Because in-patient stays have continued to get shorter, the need for beds has been reducing (although 'the absence of other elements of a community service, for example staffed hostels, will of course tend to increase the amount of in-patient care'). The psychiatric unit provides facilities for treatment on both a day and an

in-patient basis, and may act as the base from which specialist therapeutic teams provide advice and consultation outside the hospital. However psychiatrists and other health care staff, are increasingly involved in the patient's home setting and working in health centres and with primary health care teams away from their hospital base. These specialist therapeutic teams consist of psychiatrists, nurses, social workers, therapists (particularly for occupational and recreational activities) and psychologists, and service the whole district and not simply the hospital. In the White Paper the day activity area was envisaged as the hub of the psychiatric unit, with rather more than half the day hospital places used by in-patients, and the other places filled by patients coming to the hospital on a day basis. Annex 1 of the Government's Response to the Select Committee's Report envisages an adjustment to take account of falling lengths of stay, with the majority of day hospital care now provided for those outside hospital. Also

> 'in many districts it is better to site at least some of the day hospital places away from the DGH, but in a central location accessible to the community. The use of travelling day hospitals for areas with a wide geographic population distribution may be of value'.

Long-stay provision is needed for those who have been institutionalised in the past (the 'old' long-stay) as well as newly arising long-stay patients (the 'new' long-stay). In addition, the White Paper specified additional facilities specifically for the elderly. Thus each district should have a small assessment unit within the DGH with both residential and day facilities for the longer-term care of elderly mentally ill people, and these developments have been further endorsed by Annex 1 following the publication of *The Rising Tide* (ref. 45) by the Health Advisory Service.

12. In parallel and interlinked with the health service provision, there should be a range of social services facilities that is both varied and flexible.

> 'Various forms of residential accommodation are needed to cater for different degrees of dependency and for different lengths of stay. Day centres need a variety of facilities which, within a single establishment can be used flexibly to give effective help to each individual. Residential and day care services should be conceived not as a self-contained system but as part of a broad range of options – extending beyond the health and personal social services – for helping the mentally ill.'

Residential care should include short stay hostels, staffed homes, unstaffed accommodation and supervised lodgings.

13. Table A–2 shows the amounts of each service proposed in the 1975 White Paper:

Table A – 2: PROPOSED SERVICES FOR MENTALLY ILL PEOPLE
Per 100,000 population

Health:	DGH psychiatric unit (including elderly assessment unit)	:	50 beds
	Day-activity unit	:	65 places
	Long-stay elderly severely MI	:	38–45 beds
	Day care elderly severely MI	:	30–45 places
	'New' long-stay	:	To be determined
Social Services:	Short-stay hostels	:	4–6 beds
	Long-stay residential care	:	15–24 beds
	Day care	:	60 places
	Long-stay elderly MI	:	Provision in residential accommodation

In Annex 1 of the Government's Response to the Select Committee's Report, the psychiatric unit beds were subsequently reduced to 30–50 beds; and long-stay beds for elderly mentally ill people were increased to 45 beds (assuming that 15% of the population is over 65).

14. In addition, the White Paper commented on the need (without being specific about the amount) of services to provide care for people without a settled way of life; services for alcoholism; and services for drug addiction and misuse. Hence there is considerable 'vision' from the centre on the form that a community-based service should take. The White Paper model has been further developed by other contributors, such as the Richmond Fellowship (ref. 46), COHSE (ref. 47) and MIND (ref. 48). The Richmond Fellowship Working Party also described some good practice examples.

Services for Elderly People

15. Guidance on the development of community-based services for elderly people is far less specific than it is for mentally handicapped and mentally ill people. There are no indications of how the balance of care should change. The White Paper in 1981 listed services available but made no attempt to give any lead for the future. *Care in Action* set out the objectives for health authorities and local government as follows:

'(a) Strengthen the primary and community care services, together with neighbourhood and voluntary support, to enable elderly people to live at home. Some elderly people may need the additional support and cover of sheltered accommodation, in which voluntary organisations are taking an increasing interest, but this form of housing provision will be available only to relatively few

(b) Encourage an active approach to treatment and rehabilitation to enable elderly people to return to the community from hospital wherever possible. The development of acute geriatric units in district general hospitals enables acutely ill elderly people, who require the special expertise available in departments of geriatric medicine, to be cared for by a consultant in that speciality. Guidance and training aids are available to help staff improve standards of care and quality of life for in-patients in departments of geriatric medicine. These departments are centres of expertise for others involved in the care of elderly people in the hospital service and in the community

(c) Maintain capacity in the general acute sector to deal with the increasing number of elderly patients. Two-thirds of all non-psychiatric hospital in-patients aged 75 and over are currently treated in general acute beds. It is in this age group that numbers are expected to increase considerably, and in which treatment needs are generally more complex – because there may be several conditions which need treatment at the same time – and rehabilitation is more difficult than for other age groups

(d) Maintain an adequate provision for the minority of elderly people requiring long-term care in hospital or residential homes.'

Services for Younger Physically Handicapped People

16. As in the case of services for elderly people, government guidelines for services for younger physically handicapped people do not lay down amounts of service to be provided, but established a framework in which community care should develop in principle. Thus in 1970, the *Chronically Sick and Disabled Persons Act* was passed which strengthened care in the community for younger physically handicapped people in a number of ways:

(a) It required local authorities to identify younger disabled people in their areas, and to make known its services, thereby raising consciousness about the needs of this group

(b) It converted a power granted to local authorities under the 1948 *National Assistance Act* into a duty to provide practical assistance, recreational and educational facilities, help with transport, adaptations to the house, help with holiday, meals and telephones

(c) It required the provision of access and sanitary conveniences for disabled people in certain public buildings

(d) It promoted better representation for disabled people on advisory committees concerned with disability

(e) It introduced the Yellow Car Badge Scheme aimed at improving mobility and access for disabled people.

17.   In addition *Care in Action* also set out objectives for health authorities and local government as follows:

(a) Relieve pressures on caring relatives through more short-term care and treatment (including day care), development of services for the incontinent, care attendant schemes and perhaps through the development by voluntary bodies and community groups of other supporting services for disabled people and their families

(b) Further improve arrangements for caring for younger disabled people separately from elderly people

(c) Help those with hearing impairments to make the best of the improved range of aids, in particular by the recruitment and training of additional hearing therapists; and

(d) Improve co-operation between authorities to ensure that visually handicapped people, particularly elderly people, are aware of and can benefit from the services and advice which should be available to them. Services for newly blind people should be improved. They should be able to receive teaching in daily living skills and support necessary to achieve independence in the community.

JOINT PLANNING AND JOINT FINANCE

18.   The organisation required to co-ordinate and promote community care is fragmented between a range of different agencies. To overcome this fragmentation the Government introduced joint-planning arrangements. Under section 10 of the *NHS Reorganisation Act* 1973, a statutory obligation was laid on health and local authorities to co-operate in the exercise of their respective functions. Joint Consultative Committees (JCCs) were established in 1974 to advise health and local authorities

'on their performance in co-operative activities and on the planning and operation of services of common concern. It is for JCCs to identify and advise their respective authorities on the key services and client groups for which it is desirable to establish a joint approach to planning and to make recommendations year by year on priorities for joint-planning, taking account of the respective service needs and availability of manpower and money. When agreement has been reached between the authorities on the key areas for joint-planning, JCCs should prepare, for endorsement by their constituent authorities, advice on the broad strategy for further development of the relevant services, taking account of national policies, the existing pattern of local developments and the level of resources expected to be available to the health and local authority' (ref. 49).

Membership of JCCs has subsequently been extended to include representatives of housing and education authorities, family practitioner committees, and the voluntary sector.

19.   Furthermore: 'in order to develop joint-planning each health and local authority should, with advice from the JCC set up a Joint Care Planning Team (JCPT) to work at LA/HA level under the general guidance of the JCC or sub-committee. Joint-planning may require JCPTs in turn to set up specialist sub-groups' (ref. 49).

20. To help further with the promotion of joint-planning separate identified financial resources called 'joint-finance' were made available to health authorities for spending specifically on joint schemes.

'A service which is jointly-planned under the arrangements described above will generally fail to be financed by the responsible authority from its ordinary budget. The Secretary of State, however, recognises that the different methods of financing health and local authorities may hinder joint-planning. Joint financing arrangements for certain LA social services spending have therefore been introduced to ease some of the short-term difficulties which might otherwise arise locally. In essence joint-financing is designed to allow the limited and controlled use of resources available to health authorities for the purpose of supporting selected personal social services spending by local authorities (subsequently extended in 1983 to include housing and education where relevant). The criterion by which a health authority will use the money allocated to it for joint-financing will be that the spending is in the interests of the NHS as well as the local authority and can be expected to make a better contribution in terms of total care than if it directly applies to health services. Projects proposed by voluntary organisations and sponsored by the local authority may, if the authorities so wish, be financed under these arrangements'. (ref. 49 Paragraph 6).

21. As well as placing limits on the purposes for which joint-finance can be used, the Government has also issued guidelines on the pattern and duration of use. In the case of capital schemes 'in normal circumstances grants made towards the capital cost of a jointly-financed project should not exceed two-thirds of the cost. No hard and fast rules are prescribed, however, and if the JCC so recommends the whole costs may be met from NHS funds'. With regard to revenue:

- 'Health authorities may support revenue spending whether or not associated with capital projects, and revenue support of capital projects is not restricted to those which had a health authority contribution to the capital cost. All categories of revenue spending, including for example loan charges on a local authority's contribution or a jointly-financed capital scheme, are eligible for support

- The purpose of joint-finance revenue support is to help in getting the activity established, or to prevent its abandonment; but the objective in all cases will be for the local authority to assume full financial responsibility as soon as possible. It is considered essential therefore to set limits to the duration of revenue support and to require it normally to be on a tapering scale. The LA spending will need to be contained within the forecasts for the personal social services in the Government's expenditure plans published in White Papers and in the RSG settlements for the appropriate years'

Originally (1978) the duration of revenue support was relatively tightly restricted. Thus:

'Agreements for revenue support should relate initially to a period not exceeding five years; but the health authority and LA may review such agreements after three years to consider whether, in particular cases, support should be extended by a further one or two years beyond the originally agreed period – i.e. up to seven years' support for any particular project. Generally, revenue support should be on a reducing scale over the agreed period of support. But authorities may adopt a flexible attitude to the pattern of tapering'.

22. It is 'the taper' which requires authorities to 'pick up' expenditure as

time goes by that has caused major difficulties. When originally introduced local authority social services budgets were still expanding and the additional funds could be found from increasing revenue. As soon as budgets stop expanding, and in some cases started decreasing no additional money was available to pick up tapering joint-finance commitments. One result was that in 1983 the tight timescale for the taper was relaxed:

'Until the full savings accrue from the movement of people out of hospital, additional finance may be needed to match the outlay on caring for them in the community. Joint-finance can be used for this purpose and to provide the necessary flexibility Ministers have decided that in special circumstances the maximum period of joint-finance for schemes aimed at enabling people to move out of hospital may be extended to ten years at 100% and 13 years in all. DHAs may then continue the payments from their main allocations' (ref. 14).

23. As indicated in the above quote, the potential use of joint-finance for bridging was also recognised. A further development resulting from local authorities' difficulties in picking up joint-finance has been an increasing use of the funds on health service projects, with the health authority picking up the revenue consequences.

B – SOURCE AND DERIVATION OF NUMERICAL INFORMATION

The information used within the report is presented below in number order. This is followed by notes on the derivation of Exhibits (in Exhibit number order) where further detail is appropriate.

TABLE 1

PATTERN OF RESIDENTIAL CARE FUNDED BY THE PUBLIC SECTOR, 1984

NHS In-Patients – Average Number of Occupied Beds by Sector, 1984

	England	Wales	England and Wales
Geriatric*	50,300	3,800	54,100
Mental Illness	67,000	3,700	70,700
Mental Handicap	38,600	2,000	40,600
Younger Disabled Units	1,300	38	1,400

Sources: Health and Personal Social Services Statistics (HPSSS) for England 1986, Table 4.5 and HPSSS for Wales 1985, Table 4.04.

In addition to geriatric beds, people aged 65 and over in England occupy at any one time 44% or almost 50,000 acute beds and 57% or 40,000 mental illness beds. Neither group is included as Elderly In-patients within the report.

Local Authority Residential Accommodation for the Elderly and Younger Physically Handicapped, Number of Residents at 31 March 1984

	England	Wales	England and Wales
Aged under 65	4,786	398	5,184
Aged 65 and over	101,896	7,186	109,082

Sources: Health and Personal Social Services Statistics (HPSSS) for England 1986, Table 7.1 and HPSSS for Wales 1985, Table 7.01.

Local Authority Homes and Hostels for the Mentally Handicapped and Mentally Ill Residents at 31 March 1984.

	England	Wales	England and Wales
Mentally Handicapped Juniors	1,923 (2,137)	66	1,989
Mentally Handicapped Adults – Staffed	9,597 (10,663)	541	10,138
Mentally Handicapped Adults – Unstaffed	1,395 (1,550)	89	1,484
Mentally Ill People – Staffed	2,145 (2,523)	215	2,360
Mentally Ill People – Unstaffed	1,461 (1,719)	159	1,620

Sources: DHSS SR6 Division, Special Tabulation RA9A, multiplied by 0.9 to convert from places to mentally handicapped residents (places shown in brackets).
HPSSS for England 1986, Table 7.3, multiplied by 0.85 to convert from places to mentally ill residents (places shown in brackets).
Activities of Social Services Departments – Year Ended 31/3/84, Welsh Office, Tables 2.3 and 2.4.

Residents in Private and Voluntary Homes Supported by Local Authorities, 31 March 1984

	England	Wales	England and Wales
Elderly	10,307	318	10,625
Younger Physically Handicapped	3,901	201	4,102
Mentally Handicapped Juniors	395	2	397
Mentally Handicapped Adults	4,482	122	4,604
Mentally Ill	1,322	37	1,359

Sources: HPSSS for England 1986, Table 7.1 and data from SR6 Division, DHSS
Activities of Social Services Departments – Year Ended 31/3/84, Welsh Office:
Elderly and Younger Physically Handicapped, Table 1.1
Others, Table 2.2 less Table 2.1 multiplied by occupancies of 90% (MH) and 85% (MI)

Residents in Private and Voluntary Homes Supported by Supplementary Benefits (Board and Lodging Payments) at 1 December 1984

The number of Supplementary Benefit supported residents in all independent homes (including nursing homes) is obtained by multiplying the number of Board and Lodging claimants at December 1984 in England and Wales (39,900 see Table D – 6) by the proportions by category of care (April to July 1985, see Table D – 3). The *Other* and *Hospices* categories have been allocated pro rata.

	Percentage	Claimants at December 1984
Elderly	87.5%	34,900
Physically Disabled	1.5	600
Mentally Handicapped	6.2	2,500
Mentally Infirm, Alchohol and Drug Dependent	4.8	1,900

TABLE 2

PATTERN OF COMMUNITY CARE FUNDED BY THE PUBLIC SECTOR, 1984
The figures in the main report relate to 1984 and are a combination of the figures for England and Wales given below.

NHS Regular Day Patients, Average Daily Attendances by Sector

	England	Wales	England and Wales
Geriatrics	6,459	505	6,964
Mental Illness	13,118	871	13,989
Mental Handicap	1,140	123	1,263

Sources: England – DHSS Statistical Bulletin 2/86, Table 9.
Wales – HPSSS for Wales 1985, Table 8.01 and Welsh Office data for Geriatrics.

Annual attendances have been divided by 250 to give average attendances per day.

Local Authority Adult Training Centre and Day Centre Places at 31 March 1984

	England	Wales	England and Wales
ATC's for Mentally Handicapped	47,464	3,083	50,547
Day Centres for Mentally Ill	5,361	726	6,087
Day Centres for Elderly	21,492	2,181	23,673
Day Centres for YPH	9,363	385	9,748
Day Centres for Mixed Groups	16,016	1,857	17,873

For the purposes of Tables 2, 7 and 9, places in mixed centres have been allocated pro rata to the number of places in day centres for single client groups. Thus for England and Wales:

Day Centre places for Elderly People	34,400
Day Centre places for YPH	14,200
Day Centre places for Mentally Ill People	8,800

Sources: HPSSS for England 1986, Table 7.4
HPSSS for Wales 1985, Table 7.06

Local Authority Home Help Service. Number of Cases in Week Beginning 12 November 1984, England and Wales

Elderly 65 – 74	113,746
Elderly 75 +	339,428
Physically Handicapped	29,485
Mentally Handicapped	1,337
Mentally Ill	2,522
Children, Families and Other	14,954

Source: CIPFA Personal Social Services Statistics, 1984–5 Actuals, Columns 213 – 219.

Local Authority Meals Services

Meals Served Annually in Recipients' Homes 1984–5, Thousands

England	29,876
Wales	1,928

Meals Served Annually in Centres, Clubs etc, 1984–5, Thousands

England	13,055
Wales	722

Meals Served at Recipients' Homes, 4th to 10th November 1985, Wales only

Number of meals served	41,120
Number of persons receiving at least one meal	14,090
Thus, average meals per recipient per week	2.92

Sources: HPSSS for England 1986, Table 7.6
Activities of SSDs Year Ended 31/3/85 Welsh Office, Tables 5.1 and 5.2

In Table 2, the number of recipients per week in England and Wales during 1984–5 is estimated by dividing the annual number of meals served in recipients' homes by 50 (working weeks per year) and by 2.92 (the average meals per recipient, for Wales).

Other Local Authority Domiciliary Services

Assistance by SSDs in the provision of personal aids (excluding communication equipment, television and radio), 1984–5.

England	385,800
Wales	22,250

Cases of assistance by age of recipient, Wales 1984–5 (including communication equipment, television, radio and adaptations to property)

Under 16	526	(1.6%)
16 – 64	8,151	(24.5%)
65 – 74	10,252	(30.8%)
75 and over	14,377	(43.1%)

Sources: HPSSS for England 1986 Table 7.7
Activities of SSDs year ended 31/3/85, Welsh Office, Tables 6.1 and 6.2

The number of cases by age group in 1984–5 has been estimated by applying the Wales 1984–5 age breakdown (73.9% over 65) to cases of provision of personal aids.

Attendance Allowances
Numbers receiving Attendance Allowance at 31 March 1984, Great Britain

	Higher Rate	Lower Rate
Aged 2 – 64	77,000	118,000
Aged 65 – 74	36,000	46,000

Source: Social Security Statistics 1985, Table 14.30.

The England and Wales figures in Table 2 have been obtained by multiplying the above figures by 0.906 to reflect the proportion of total Great Britain population in England and Wales.

TABLE 3

EXPENDITURE BY CLIENT GROUP, 1984–5

Programme Budget, Gross Current Expenditure, England, 1984–5

Hospital and Community Health Services

	Base	With Overheads
Elderly		
Geriatric In-patients	£795.0 m	
Geriatric Out-patients	7.0	
Chiropody	28.3	
Non Psychiatric Day Patients (75%)	43.4	
District Nursing (44%)	117.6	
	991.3	1,057
Younger Disabled		
Units for Younger Disabled	18.5	
Non Psychiatric Day Patients (25%)	14.4	
District Nursing (6%)	16.0	
	48.9	52
Mentally Handicapped		
Mental Handicap In-patients	460.8	
Mental Handicap Out-patients	0.8	
Psychiatric Day Patients (8%)	5.2	
	466.8	498
Mentally Ill		
Mental Illness In-patients	900.9	
Mental Illness Out-patients	62.1	
Psychiatric Day Patients (92%)	60.4	
	1,023.4	1,091

Source: Fourth Report from the Social Services Committee, Session 1985–6, Volume II, Table 3.1

The study assumes that 44% of *District Nursing* expenditure relates to elderly people, on the basis of the age profile of all clients nursed. Furthermore, the study assumes that one half of *District Nursing* expenditure relates to the priority groups, and the balance of this (6%) is allocated to younger disabled people.

Expenditure on *Pyschiatric Day Patients* has been split between mentally handicapped and the mentally ill people according to the relative numbers of day patients *(DHSS Mental Health Statistics for England 1984)*.

The figures in the right hand column show an on-cost of 6.6% to allow for *Other Community Health Services* and *HQ Administration* expressed as a percentage of all other expenditure.

Personal Social Services (including Joint Finance)

	Base	With Overheads
Elderly		
Residential	£626.9 m	
Day Care	57.7	
Home Helps (90%)	268.9	
Meals	53.6	
Aids, Adaptations etc (74%)	25.8	
	1032.9	1,378
Younger Physically Handicapped		
Residential	52.3	
Day Care	23.1	
Home Helps (6%)	17.9	
Aids, Adaptations etc (26%)	9.0	
	102.3	136
Mentally Handicapped		
Residential Adults	98.4	
Residential Children	36.2	
Day Care ATC's	106.6	
	241.2	322
Mentally Ill		
Residential	21.0	
Day Care	18.0	
Home Helps (1%)	3.0	
	42.0	56

Source: Fourth Report from the Social Services Committee, Session 1985–6, Volume II, Table 3.1

The division of expenditure on *Home Helps* and *Aids, Adaptations etc.* between client groups is based on the CIPFA data referred to in the notes to Exhibits 3, 4 and 5.

In addition to the expenditure in the left hand column the study assumes that one half of *Social Work* expenditure (£160.8 million) relates to the priority groups. This has been allocated pro rata to expenditure by client groups giving an on-cost of 11.3%. *Other Local Authority Expenditure, Local Authority Administration* and *Training* have been allocated pro rata to expenditure, representing a further overhead factor of 19.9%. The right hand column includes both these elements, representing a combined on-cost of 33.4%.

Social Security Expenditure

Figures provided by the DHSS (see notes to Exhibit 11) give the following expenditure for Great Britain in 1984–5

Attendance Allowance (AA)	£576 million
Invalid Care Allowance (ICA)	11
Supplementary Benfit B & L (Independent Homes) at December	200

Expenditure on AA and ICA has been divided between England (86%) and the remainder of Great Britain according to overall population. Supplementary Benefits board and lodging (B & L) expenditure has been divided between England and Wales according to population, and to Scotland on the basis of Table D–3 (Appendix D); overall this implies that 90% of expenditure relates to England.

The expenditure has been allocated to client groups according to the following percentages:

	AA and ICA	B & L
Elderly	59%	87%
Mentally Handicapped	4	6
Mentally Ill	–	5
Younger Physically Handicapped	37	2

This gives the following expenditure for England by client group:

	AA	ICA	B & L	Total
Elderly	£292 m	6	157	455
Mentally Handicapped	20	–	11	31
Mentally Ill	–	–	9	9
Younger Physically Handicapped	183	4	4	191

Expenditure for England and Wales in 1986–7

The expenditure figures for England in 1984–5 that are presented in Table 3 have been updated to November 1986 through the following assumptions. NHS and PSS expenditure has been increased by 9% to allow for general price inflation. Social security expenditure has been increased in line with Exhibit 11:

Attendance Allowance   +   34%
Invalid Care Allowance + 800%
Board and Lodging   + 144%

The expenditure figures have been increased by a further 6% to allow for Wales. This gives the following expenditure by agency across all priority groups:

NHS   £3.1 million
PSS   2.2
Social Security   1.3

TABLE 4

COSTS OF CARE IN DIFFERENT SETTINGS, 1986
For the source of figures in Table 4, see Tables 20 and 21.

TABLE 5

PROGRESS TO WHITE PAPER TARGETS FOR MENTALLY HANDICAPPED PEOPLE
The 1969 data is from Table 5 in 'Better Services for the Mentally Handicapped' (Cmmd 4683), 1971.

Available Adult Beds
The 1984 figures are derived as follows:

Resident Patients aged over 16, England	36,936
Resident Patients aged over 16, Wales	1,902
Thus, Ratio of Adult Patients England and Wales: England	1.053:1
Total Available Beds, England	41,143
% Residents aged over 16, England	98.0%
Thus, Available Adult Beds, England	40,320
Thus, Available Adult Beds, England and Wales	42,500

Sources: Mental Health Statistics for England 1984, Booklet 10, Table 1.1
          HPSSS for Wales 1985, Table 8.13

Adult Residential Places, March 1984

	England	Wales
Local Authority Staffed/Unstaffed	12,213	700
Private and Voluntary	5,220	400
Total	17,433	1,100

Sources: DHSS SR6 Division, Special Tabulation RA9A and RA9B.
Activities of SSD's, year ended March 1984, Welsh Office, Tables 2.4 and 2.5 (divided by 0.9 to convert to places)

Local Authority Adult Training Centre Places at 31 March 1984

England	47,464
Wales	3,083
	50,547

Sources: HPSSS for England 1986, Table 7.4
HPSSS for Wales 1985, Table 7.06

Targets for 1991

	Rate/100,000	England and Wales	England only
Available Adult In-Patient Beds	55	27,300	25,800
Residential Adult Places	60	29,800	28,200
Local Authority ATC places	150	74,500	70,500
Hospital Day Patients	10	5,000	4,700

Sources: Rates per 100,000 population are from 'Better Services for the Mentally Handicapped' (Cmnd. 4683), Table 5. ATC's places include all places in the community for adults living in the community (130/100,000) and adults coming by day from hospital (20/100,000). The total requirement is obtained by multiplying the rate by the 1984 population of England and Wales (49.7 million), and England only (47 million).

TABLE 6

BALANCE OF EXPENDITURE FOR MENTALLY HANDICAPPED PEOPLE

The balance of expenditure in Table 6 is derived from the Programme Budget for England as presented in Table 3.1 of the Fourth Report from the Social Services Committee, Session 1985–6, Volume II. The calculation of each figure is shown in the table below.

	1976–7	1984–5	Factor to Target	Target
Mental Handicap In-patients	£427.0 m	460.8	25.8:40.3	295.0
Psychiatric Day Patients (8%)	3.1	5.2	4.7: 1.3	18.8
Mental Handicap Out-patients	0.5	0.8	1.0	0.8
NHS Total	430.6	466.8		314.6
NHS including Overhead	464.2	497.6		335.4
(overhead factor)	(+7.8%)	(+6.6%)		
Residential MH Adults	47.1	98.4	28.2:17.4	159.5
Day Care ATC	76.5	106.6	70.5:47.5	158.2
Social Workers	12.6	23.2		35.9
(social work factor)	(10.2%)	(11.3%)		
LA Total	136.2	228.2		353.6
LA including Overhead	164.4	273.6		424.0
(overhead factor)	(+20.7%)	(+19.9%)		
TOTAL	628.6	771.2		759.2%
% NHS	73.8%	64.5%		44.5%
Total Residential	517.2	609.2		505.7
% Residential	82.3%	79.0%		66.6%

The first two columns come directly from the Social Services Committee report with the following exceptions (the assumptions being consistent with those for Table 3):

- 8% of *Psychiatric Day Patient* expenditure is included
- The NHS overhead is included to allow for *Other Community Health Service* expenditure and *HQ Administration*
- One half of social workers expenditure is assumed to apply to the priority groups and this is allocated between them pro rata to total LA expenditure on the client group (an on-cost of 10.2% in 1976–7 and 11.3% in 1984–5)
- The LA overhead is included to allow for *Other LA, LA Administration* and *Training*.

The 1984–5 totals differ from those in Table 3 because local authority residential care for mentally handicapped children has been excluded.

The total expenditure on residential care is taken to be the sum of Mental Handicapped *In-Patient* and Local Authority *Residential* expenditure plus their overheads (though excluding the *Social Worker* on-cost).

The final column of the table is obtained by multiplying the 1984–5 expenditure by factors to represent the distance from the White Paper targets for 1991. These factors which relate to England only, are taken from the notes to Table 5. The factor for *Day Patients* is based on 1300 places (see notes to Table 12) compared to the target of 4700. All costs are in 1984–5 prices after allowing for pay and price inflation.

TABLE 7 PROGRESS TO WHITE PAPER TARGETS FOR MENTALLY ILL PEOPLE

Hospital In-Patient Beds and Day Places

	1974	1984
Average daily available beds	104,400	78,900
Regular day patient attendances/day	8,964	13,563
Day hospital places	11,233	16,996

Sources: DHSS Statistical Bulletin 2/86, Tables 2 and 9 (Annual day patient attendances have been divided by 250 to give attendances per day, and the 1974 figure multipled by 92% to exclude mental handicap patients). Day hospital places in 1984 are from Table 3 of Mental Health Statistics for England 1984, Booklet 9. They include places for in-patients and people living in the community. Day hospital places in 1974 has been derived from attendances per day by applying the 1984 occupancy factor (13,563/16,996 = 79.8%).

Places in Residential Homes at 31 March

	1974	1984
Local Authority Staffed homes	1,716	2,523
Local Authority Unstaffed homes	482	1,723
Private and Voluntary homes	1,350	2,558
Total Places	3,548	6,804

Source: HPSSS for England 1985, Table 7.3

Day Centre Places for the Mentally Ill at 31 March

	1974	1984
Local Authority Centres		
Centres for Mentally Ill People	3,598	5,361
Places in Mixed Centres	913	2,371
Total Local Authority Places	4,511	7,732
Voluntary and Other Places	893	1,225
Total Places	5,404	8,957

Sources: DHSS Local Authority Statistics A/F84/8, Table 2 and form SSDA 512. The places for the Mentally Ill in mixed centres has been determined by allocating places pro rata to the number of places for the elderly, younger physically handicapped and mentally ill in other centres (see notes to Table 9).

	Rates per 100,000	England Total
In-patient Beds		
District General Hospitals	50	
Accommodation for Elderly Severely Mentally Infirm	35	
Units for the 'New' Long-Stay	17	
	102	47,900
Day Hospital Places		
District General Hospitals	65	
Elderly Severely Mentally Infirm	32.5	
	97.5	45,800
Residential Places		
Hostels	5.0	
Long-stay Accommodation	19.5	
	24.5	11,500
Day Centre Places	60	28,200

Sources: 'Better Services for the Mentally Ill' (Cmnd. 6233) 1975, paragraph 4.64. The mid-points of quoted ranges have been adopted. The totals for England have been calculated using the population in 1984 (47 million).

TABLE 8

BALANCE OF EXPENDITURE FOR MENTALLY ILL PEOPLE

The balance of expenditure in Table 8 is derived from the Programme Budget in a similar fashion to Table 6. The calculations are summarised below, which should be interpreted using the notes to Table 6.

	1976–7	1984–5	Factor to Target	Target
Mental Illness In-patients	£839.6 m	900.9	47.9:78.9	546.9
Psychiatric Day Patients (92%)	35.6	60.4	45.8:17.0	162.7
Mental Illness Out-patients	39.5	62.1	1.0	62.1
NHS Total	914.7	1,023.4		771.7
NHS including Overhead	986.0	1,090.9		822.6
(overhead factor)	(+7.8%)	(+6.6%)		
Residential M Illness	14.5	21.0	11.5:6.8	35.5
Day Care M Illness	8.8	18.0	28.2:9.0	56.4
Social Workers	2.4	4.4		10.4
(social work factor)	(10.2%)	(11.3%)		
LA Total	25.7	43.4		102.3
LA including Overhead	31.0	52.0		122.7
(overhead factor)	(+20.7%)	(19.9%)		
Total	1,017.0	1,142.9		945.3
% NHS	97.0%	95.5%		87.0%
Total Residential	922.6	985.5		625.6
% Residential	90.7%	86.2%		66.2%

TABLE 9

BALANCE OF CARE FOR ELDERLY PEOPLE

Hospital In-Patient Beds and Day Patients

	1974	1979	1984
Average daily number of occupied geriatric beds			
England	51,100	50,700	50,300
Wales	3,500	3,800	3,800
	54,600	54,500	54,100
Average daily number of regular day patients in geriatrics			
England	3,804	4,670	6,459
Wales	275	318	505
	4,079	4,988	6,964

Sources: DHSS Statistical Bulletin 2/86 Tables 3 and 9.
HPSSS for Wales 1985 Table 4.02 and additional data from the Welsh Office.

The annual number of day patients has been divided by 250 days to give an average daily number of attendances.

Residential Homes, Residents at 31 March, aged 65 and over

	1974	1979	1984
Local Authority Homes			
England	92,462	102,086	101,996
Wales	6,172	7,031	7,186
	98,634	109,117	109,182
Voluntary Homes			
England	22,708	24,716	26,005
Wales	633	882	890
	23,341	25,598	26,895
Private Homes			
England	18,926	26,095	52,675
Wales	357	745	2,330
	19,283	26,840	55,005

Sources: DHSS Local Authority Statistics RA/83/2, Table D and RA/84/2, Table G.
HPSSS for Wales 1985, Tables 7.01 and 7.04. Earlier years from the Welsh Office (1979 figures by interpolation between 1978 and 1980)

Registered Nursing Homes

	1974	1979	1984
England			
Registered Beds All			
Specialties	26,965	31,361	–
Long-stay Beds for Elderly	13,482	15,680	27,346
Occupied Beds for Elderly	11,450	13,350	23,250
Wales			
Long-Stay Beds for Elderly	–	–	1,031
Occupied Beds for Elderly	450	500	900
England and Wales			
Occupied Beds for Elderly	11,900	13,800	24,100

Sources: Registered Beds 1974 and 1979 – 'Private Health Care, 1985', Office of Health Economics, Table 4.5 (1979 by Interpolation)
Beds for Elderly – 1984 data provided by DHSS and Welsh Office from SBH 212 returns. Data for earlier years assumes 50% of all beds
Occupied beds – England all years and Wales 1984 assumes 85% occupancy. Wales for 1974 and 1979 assumes the number of occupied beds to be 4% of that for England (it being the 1984 ratio).

Local Authority Day Centre Places at 31 March

	1974	1979	1984
England			
Day Centres for Elderly People	10,058	18,889	21,492
Day Centres for Mixed Groups of which:	5,818	12,307	16,016
Elderly	2,552	6,905	9,504
YPH	2,353	3,712	4,141
Mentally Ill	913	1,690	2,371
Wales			
Day Centres for Elderly People	795	2,525	2,181
Day Centres for Mixed Groups of which:	766	886	1,857
Elderly	364	749	1,230
YPH	335	154	217
Mentally Ill	67	93	410
All places for Elderly People			
England	12,610	25,794	30,996
Wales	1,159	3,274	3,411
	13,769	29,068	34,407

Sources: DHSS Local Authority Statistics A/F83/8, Table 2
HPSSS for England 1986, Table 7.4
HPSSS for Wales 1985, Table 7.06 (earlier years from the Welsh Office)

The places in mixed day centres have been allocated to the three client groups pro rata to the number of places available in centres for single client groups in the same year.

Home Help Staff and Organisers, Whole-time equivalents at 30 September

	1974	1979	1984
England	42,388	46,714	53,149
Wales	2,798	2,914	3,573
	45,186	49,628	56,722

Sources: DHSS Local Authority Statistics S/F85/1, Table C
HPSSS for Wales 1985, Table 3.24 (earlier years from the Welsh Office)

Meals Service, thousands of meals provided in recipients homes and elsewhere

	1974	1979	1984
England	33,575	40,949	42,373
Wales	1,614	2,372	2,615
	35,189	43,321	44,988

Sources: DHSS Local Authority Statistics A/F83/11, Table 1
HPSSS for England 1986, Table 7.6
HPSSS for Wales 1985, Table 7.08 (earlier years from the Welsh Office)

Population Aged 75 and Over, mid-year estimates

	1974	1979	1984
England	2,327,600	2,619,200	2,986,000
Wales	140,600	158,900	181,400
	2,468,200	2,778,100	3,167,400

Source: Figures provided by the Population Estimates Unit of the Office of Population Censuses and Surveys.

TABLE 10

COSTS OF RESIDENTIAL HOMES FOR THE ELDERLY
Gross Cost per Resident Week, 1985

	Lowest	Mean	Highest
Local Authority Homes	£85.85	110.90	185.12
Private Homes	36.30	117.30	247.20
Voluntary Homes	21.20	90.20	202.10

Sources: Personal Social Services Statistics 1984–85 Actuals, CIPFA, Column 179 (gross cost per resident week excluding capital charges). For the derivation of the mean local authority cost see Table 20. 'Survey of Private and Voluntary Residential and Nursing Homes for the DHSS', Ernst & Whinney, Table 6.

TABLE 11

TYPICAL COSTS, 1986
See tables 20 and 21

TABLE 12

COMPARISON OF THE COST OF THE WHITE PAPER PROPOSAL VERSUS CURRENT PROVISION

Figures on actual and White Paper provision are taken from the notes to Table 5 (England only) and from Table 7 with the exception of hospital day patient places for the mentally handicapped people:

	England	Wales	England and Wales
Day Patient Attendances	291,000	30,846	321,800
Attendances per day	1,164	123	1,287
Available places	1,293	137	1,430

Sources: Attendances – DHSS Statistical Bulletin 2/86, Table 9 and HPSSS for Wales 1985, Table 8.01
Attendances per day – attendances divided by 250 days
Available places – attendances per day divided by 90% occupancy

Figures on expenditure are taken from the notes to Table 6 and Table 8.

TABLE 13

COST TO LOCAL RATEPAYERS OF AN ADDITIONAL £1 MILLION OF EXPENDITURE
Source: Audit Commission Local Authority Profiles 1986–7

TABLE 14

LOCAL AUTHORITY STAFF CHANGES – 1983 TO 1986
Source: Joint Manpower Watch for England. March 1986 return in DOE Press Notice 325, June 1986.

TABLE 15

JOINT FINANCE EXPENDITURE
£ million

Year	Capital	Revenue	Total	PSS Revaluer	Capital	Revenue	Total
	(at outturn prices)				(at 1984–5 prices)		
1976–7	3.0	1.2	4.2	2.222	6.6	2.7	9.3
1977–8	8.9	8.6	17.5	2.027	18.1	17.4	35.5
1978–9	15.5	15.6	31.1	1.871	29.0	29.2	48.2
1979–80	16.4	23.4	39.8	1.587	26.0	37.1	63.1
1980–1	23.2	36.9	60.1	1.320	30.6	48.7	79.3
1981–2	23.6	49.2	72.8	1.174	27.7	57.8	85.5
1982–3	26.4	56.7	83.1	1.096	28.9	62.1	91.0
1983–4	21.4	66.3	87.7	1.039	22.2	68.9	91.1
1984–5	22.4	74.2	96.6	1.0	22.4	74.2	96.6

Sources: Expenditure at outturn prices for years to 1982–3 from 'Progress in Partnership: Report of the Working Group on Joint Planning', Annex D.
Expenditure for 1983–4 and 1984–5 from RHA summarised accounts.
PSS revaluer provided by FA1 division, DHSS

TABLE 16

NHS AND LOCAL AUTHORITY EXPENDITURE ON MENTAL HEALTH

Table 16 is derived directly from the programme budget figures for England that are presented in the notes to Table 6 and Table 8.

TABLE 17

SUPPLEMENTARY BENEFIT PAYMENTS FOR BOARD AND LODGING – MAXIMUM LIMITS
Source: DHSS Press Release 86/195, June 1986

TABLE 18
DHSS ESTIMATES OF SOCIAL SECURITY BENEFITS
See Exhibit 11 and Appendix C

TABLE 19
EFFECT OF RAWP AND CHANGES IN SB PAYMENTS, 1977 TO 1985

RAWP Gain per Head of Weighted Population

The derivation of the *RAWP Gain* by RHA is derived according to the table below. Columns 1 and 2 show the 'weighted' population of each RHA, aggregated across the six service categories for 1977–8 and 1985–6. They show the relative need across regions for resources allocated through RAWP, constrained to the national population.

Columns 3 and 5 show the RAWP general allocation to each RHA in 1977–8 and 1985–6. Column 4 expresses the 1977–8 allocation in 1985–6 prices according to the Hospital and Community Health Services revaluer (assuming 6% inflation between 1984–5 and 1985–6).

Columns 6 and 7 show these allocations divided by weighted population of each RHA. If all RHAs were 'at target' their allocations per capita would equal the aggregate figure for England.

Column 8 is the difference between Columns 6 and 7. The England total gain (£22.89 per capita) represents the additional resources that have been made available nationally to allow for demographic changes (e.g. the increasing proportion of elderly people) and service development. The regional variation about this figure represents 'gains' and 'losses' brought about by RHAs moving closer to their targets.

RHA	Aggregated Weighted Populations '000		RAWP Allocation 1977–8	1977–8 at 1985–6 Prices	RAWP Allocation 1985–6	RAWP Allocation Per Capita		Gain Per Capita
	1977–8	1985–6				1977–8	1985–6	
	1	2	3	4	5	6	7	8
Northern	3,256	3,215	£ 219.0m	£ 502.8m	£ 601.5m	£154.40	£187.11	£32.71
Yorkshire	3,553	3,621	251.7	577.9	676.1	162.66	186.71	24.05
Trent	4,282	4,414	287.8	660.8	810.7	154.32	183.69	29.37
E Anglia	1,751	1,862	122.8	281.9	345.7	160.94	185.67	24.73
NW Thames	3,376	3,309	293.4	673.7	686.5	199.58	207.46	7.88
NE Thames	3,792	3,998	325.0	746.1	853.5	196.74	213.46	16.72
SE Thames	3,673	3,704	310.2	712.2	756.2	193.88	204.15	10.27
SW Thames	3,132	2,930	246.9	567.0	590.1	181.04	201.37	20.33
Wessex	2,557	2,660	177.9	408.4	491.5	159.76	184.74	24.98
Oxford	1,848	2,058	146.6	336.6	386.1	182.15	187.64	5.49
S Western	3,100	3,155	218.5	501.6	594.1	161.84	188.28	26.44
W Midlands	4,958	5,133	345.5	793.2	944.4	159.99	183.99	24.00
Mersey	2,655	2,528	189.2	434.5	486.6	163.67	192.50	28.83
N Western	4,485	4,365	299.1	686.8	826.1	153.15	189.26	36.11
TOTAL	46,418	46,952	3,433.6	7,883.6	9,049.1	169.84	192.73	22.89

SB Gain per Head of Population

The *Supplementary Benefit Gain* is estimated on the basis that the payments for board and lodging (B & L) are distributed pro rata to Private and Voluntary residents aged 65 and over. The total expenditure on B & L payments for England and Wales in December 1985 is assumed to be £316 million (see below).

RHA	P&V Residents 65 & over	SB 'Gain'	Weighted Population 000's	SB 'Gain' per head
Northern	3,123	£ 10.4m	3,215	£ 3.22
Yorkshire	6,245	20.7	3,621	£ 5.72
Trent	4,985	16.5	4,414	£ 3.75
East Anglia	4,245	14.1	1,862	£ 7.56
NW Thames	4,616	15.3	3,309	£ 4.63
NE Thames	5,048	16.7	3,998	£ 4.19
SE Thames	10,391	34.5	3,704	£ 9.31
SW Thames	9,438	31.3	2,930	£10.69
Wessex	9,111	30.2	2,660	£11.36
Oxford	3,363	11.2	2,058	£ 5.42
South Western	12,632	41.9	3,155	£13.28
West Midlands	6,530	21.7	5,133	£ 4.22
Mersey	4,065	13.5	2,528	£ 5.33
North Western	7,723	25.6	4,365	£ 5.87
England Total	91,515	303.8	46,952	£ 6.47

Sources:

Col 1   P & V residents 65+ by local authority at 31 March 1985 provided by SR6 Division, DHSS June 1986. Corrected for reported errors in respect of Kensington and Chelsea LB and Liverpool. Local authorities straddling RHA boundaries have been allocated pro rata to population.

Col 2   Column 1 has been multiplied by £316 million (Audit Commission December 1985 estimate for England and Wales, see Appendix D) and divided by 95,560 (P&V residents 65+ at March 1985, England and Wales corrected).

Col 3   Aggregated weighted population by Region for 1985–6, see above.

Col 4   By division (col 2/col 3)

TABLES 20 AND 21

Cost to Social Security

ILLUSTRATIVE COSTS

State Pension, Attendance Allowance (lower rate), and Severe Disablement Allowance at July 1986 rates.

Housing Benefit: All figures with the following exception were supplied by DHSS, as being representative of the type of accommodation. The housing benefit figure for group homes (in Table 21) assumes one half of gross costs are recovered through housing benefit (see below).

Supplementary Benefit: (at July 1986 rates)

Table 20 options (i) to (iii) difference between *SB Long-term Householder Rate plus Heating Allowance* and *State Pension*.

(v) difference between P & V *Residential Home Board and Lodging Maximum plus Personal Allowance*, and the *State Pension plus Attendance Allowance;*

(vi) as (v), using P & V *Nursing Home Board and Lodging Maximum)*

Table 21 option (a) difference between *Non-householder Long-term SB Rate* and *Severe Disablement Allowance*.

(b) as (a) plus 25% of the difference between *Householder* and *Non-householder Long-term Rates*.

(c) difference between *Maximum Ordinary Board and Lodging Rate plus Personal Allowance* and the *Severe Disablement Allowance*.

(d) difference between *Statutory Minimum Charge plus Personal Allowance,* and the *Severe Disablement Allowance*.

(e) difference between P and V *Residential Home Board and Lodging Maximum plus Personal Allowances* and the *Severe Disablement Allowance*.

Cost to NHS

Home care (Table 20) – the following assumption has been made:

The person in their own home receives one visit per week from a nurse (or other community health worker) at an average cost to the health authority of £4.00 (November 1986 prices).

In-patient care by hospital type:

	Cost per day 1984–5 costs	Cost per Week	
		1984–5 costs	November 1986 prices
Mental Handicap Hospitals	£32.43	227	247
Geriatric Hospitals	37.60	263	287

Sources: Fourth Report from the Social Services Committee Session 1985–6 Volume II – actual figures provided by DHSS. 1984–5 costs have been increased by 9% to bring them in line with November 1986 prices.

Cost to SSD

Domiciliary Table 20 – it is assumed that in options (i) to (iii) the client receives: 2.5 hours of home help at a net cost to the authority of £3.30 per hour (November 1986 prices), and other domiciliary services (meals, aids, adaptions, holidays etc.) at an average cost of £3.75 per week (November 1986 prices).

Table 21 – the cost to the local authority (or health authority) is calculated as one visit per day at £4 per visit in option (a), two visits per week per client in option (b) and one visit per week per client in option (c).

Source: (Table 20): CIPFA Personal Social Services Statistics 1984–5 Actuals. Figure for other domiciliary services is sum of net expenditure on meals and community services divided by an estimate of 440,000 clients (see note to Table 2).

Day Centres and Training Centres – Average Gross Cost per Place for Local Authority Day Care (England only).

	Cost per Annum 1984–5 costs	Cost per Week	
		1984–5 costs	November 1986 prices
Day centres	£1,817	35	38
Adult Training centres	2,184	42	46

Source: As hospital in-patient costs above.

Residential Homes – Average Gross Cost per Resident in Local Authority Homes (England only).

	Cost per Annum 1984–5 costs	Cost per Week	
		1984–5 costs	November 1986 prices
Mentally Handicapped adults	£6,302	121.20	132
Elderly and Younger Physically handicapped	5,767	110.90	121

Source: As hospital in-patients costs above.

Local Authority Group Homes for Mentally Handicapped People

	Gross	Net
Average annual cost/place (1984–5)	£1,354	677
Average weekly cost/place (1984–5)	26	13
Average weekly cost/place (November 1986 prices)	28	14

Source: CIPFA Personal Social Services Statistics, 1984–85 Actuals. Based on three authorities for which full information was available.

Cost to Housing Department

HRA deficit on sheltered housing from Audit Commission Housing Supervision and Management Survey, November 1984:
- – Average cost of services for the elderly was £263 per dwelling per annum
- – Service charges to the elderly were £24 per dwelling per annum
The net annual cost to Housing Revenue Accounts was £239 (1983–4 prices) which is equivalent to £5.20 per week at November 1986 prices.

Cost to DOE

The cost of rate relief for disabled persons is taken to be £84 per year (1984–5), or £1.60 per week at November 1986 prices, for those in their own homes. For those in residential care the average annual cost per institution, £3,400 (1984–5) is divided by 16 persons to give an average weekly cost of £4.50 at November 1986 prices.

TABLE 22

STAFFING TRENDS 1974 TO 1984
England only. Whole-time equivalents

Local Authority Staff at 30 September

	1974	1979	1984
Residential Care for Adults	48,774	56,790	64,242
Day Care for Adults (including ATC's)	8,058	11,356	15,035
Home Help Service	42,388	46,713	53,145
Other Community Support	1,354	1,600	2,204
OT's included above	N/A	N/A	893
Social Workers	17,042	22,734	24,292

Source: DHSS Local Authority Statistics S/F85/1, Table C.

NHS Nursing Staff at 30 September

	1974	1979	1984
Mental Illness Hospitals and Units	42,976	50,305	57,555
of which CPN's	N/A	1,148	2,234
Mental Handicap Hospitals and Units	21,030	25,774	30,039
District Nurses	10,827	13,738	15,174

Sources: Mental Health Statistics for England 1984, Booklet 9, Table 7 and Booklet 10, Table 7. (Earlier years from DHSS SR2C division).
HPSSS for England 1986, Table 6.6

TABLE 23

COST OF SERVICES FOR MENTALLY HANDICAPPED PEOPLE IN PLYMOUTH
Source: Figures supplied by Devon County Council staff.

EXHIBITS 3, 4 and 5

GROSS EXPENDITURE BY LOCAL AUTHORITY
All data is gross expenditure from the CIPFA Personal Social Services Statistics, 1984–5 Actuals. Expenditure has been allocated to the four client groups: Elderly, Younger Physically Handicapped (YPH), Mentally Handicapped Adults (MHA) and Mentally Ill (MI) people as shown below.
Own Residential Homes – expenditure on homes for a single client group has been allocated directly. Expenditure on mixed homes has been allocated pro rata to national expenditure on own adult homes (ie Elderly 85.7%, YPH 2.5%, MHA 9.5%, MI 2.3%).
Other Residential Homes – allocated to the client group identified.
Group Homes – allocated to MHA or MI, as identified.
Own and Other Day Centres – single client group centres allocated directly.

Mixed centres allocated pro rata to national expenditure on single group centres (ie Elderly 48.9%, YPH 32.0%, MHA 4.8%, MI 14.3%). All Sheltered Employment expenditure has been allocated to YPH, and all Adult Training Centres expenditure has been allocated to MHA.

Home Help Service – where individual authorities have provided a breakdown of cases by client group for the week beginnning 12 November 1984 this has been used to split home help gross expenditure by client group. For other authorities the national split of cases by client group has been used (ie Elderly 90.5%, YPH 5.8%, MHA 0.3%, MI 0.5%, Families and Other 2.9%).

Other Domiciliary Services – Expenditure on meals has been allocated entirely to the Elderly. Expenditure on Aids, Adaptations, Telephones, Holidays etc. has been divided between Elderly (73.9%) and YPH (26.1%) according to the age breakdown of those receiving assistance. Expenditure by social services departments on sheltered housing has been allocated to the Elderly.

Other Expenditure – expenditure unallocated to the above services has been allocated to client groups where specified. *Other Expenditure* on mixed client groups has been allocated between adult client groups pro rata to *Other Expenditure* on single client groups (ie Elderly 38.4%, YPH 49.5%, MHA 5.1%, MI 7.0%). *Grants to Voluntary Organisations* has been allocated in a similar fashion, the allocations for mixed client groups being (Elderly 47.2%, YPH 37.1%, MHA 5.5%, MI 10.2%).

Expenditure on the following activities has not been included:
Management and Central Services
Research and Development
Fieldwork
Children
Mentally Handicapped Children.

EXHIBIT 6   HOME HELP SERVICE BY LOCAL AUTHORITY

All data is from CIPFA Personal Social Services Statistics, 1984–5 Actuals. The number of home help full-time equivalents includes: home help organisers, assistant and trainee home help organisers, home helps and other domiciliary support staff. The proportion of expenditure on elderly people that is on the home help service is calculated by dividing the gross expenditure on home helps that is attributable to elderly people, by total social services department expenditure attributable to elderly people. Both figures are calculated as discussed under Exhibit 3.

EXHIBIT 7   ELDERLY RESIDENTS IN PRIVATE AND VOLUNTARY HOMES

The number of elderly residents in private and voluntary homes (by authority) is the number of residents aged 65 and over in residential homes for elderly and younger physically handicapped people, at 31 March 1985. The unpublished data were provided by SR6 Division of DHSS, based on RA3 returns. Corrections have been made in respect of two authorities (Kensington and Chelsea and Liverpool) as discussed in Appendix D.

The number of elderly residents in private and voluntary homes in each authority has been divided by the population aged 75 and over using the OPCS estimates for 30 June 1984. For presentation purposes Metropolitan Districts and London Boroughs have been aggregated into county areas.

EXHIBIT 8

TOTAL RESIDENTIAL CARE FOR THE ELDERLY

The number of elderly residents in private and voluntary homes is defined in the same way as for Exhibit 7.

The number of elderly residents in local authority homes is the number of the local authority's own clients aged 65 and over, who are resident in the authority's own accommodation at 31 March 1985.(Column 168 of Personal Social Services Statistics 1984–5 Actuals, CIPFA). In the case of authorities for which the above data is unavailable, the number of resident weeks during the financial year (column 173) has been divided by 52.

In each case the number of residents has been divided by the population aged 75 and over at 30 June 1984.

EXHIBIT 9

CHANGING COST TO RATEPAYERS OF DIFFERENT STRATEGIES

The illustrative costs are based on the illustrative example of Table 21. For somebody discharged from hospital (annual cost £13,000 although full savings are only realised when the hospital closes) into a group home with domiciliary support and attendance at a training centre five days a week, the cost to local authorities is £3,500 per annum (using average rather than marginal costs). If grant lost is £1 for every £1 extra spending the cost to the local authority is £7,000 per annum. If a transfer package is negotiated to cover the cost, the £3,500 may be provided by the health authority and the placement does not cost the local authority any increase. If the health authority provide a standard sum (e.g. half the hospital cost equivalent to £6,500 say), the local authority makes a 'profit' of £3,000 which then saves it a further £3,000 in extra grant or £6,000 in total.

EXHIBIT 10

NHS IN-PATIENT COSTS
England £ million at 1984–5 Prices (after allowing for pay and price inflation)

Financial Year	In-Patient Costs	Annual Cost per occupied bed	Average Daily Occupied beds (inc. MH Units) calendar year
Mental Handicap Hospitals			
1976–7	£427.0 m	£8,748	48,800
1977–8	444.8	9,218	47,900
1978–9	451.2	9,693	46,600
1979–80	450.5	9,817	45,400
1980–1	453.3	10,207	44,100
1981–2	460.1	10,718	43,000
1982–3	464.9	11,117	41,600
1983–4	461.9	11,342	40,300
1984–5	460.8	11,837	38,600
Mental Illness Hospitals			
1976–7	839.6	10,027	83,800
1977–8	874.3	10,752	80,800
1978–9	874.8	11,215	78,200
1979–80	880.1	11,379	76,500
1980–1	892.6	11,792	75,200
1981–2	906.6	12,209	73,400
1982–3	901.7	12,582	71,300
1983–4	898.3	12,813	69,300
1984–5	900.9	13,315	67,000

Sources: In-patient Costs – Fourth Report from the Social Services Committee, Session 1985–86, Volume II, Table 3.1

Annual cost per occupied bed – Fourth Report from the Social Services Committee, Session 1985–86, Volume II Chart 3.2 (actual figures supplied by FA1C Division, DHSS). Cost per day multiplied by 365 days.

Average daily occupied beds – DHSS Statistical Bulletin 2/86, Table 3. Figures relate to calendar years and include specialist units within other hospitals.

EXHIBIT 11

TRENDS IN SOCIAL SECURITY PAYMENTS
Great Britain, £million

Financial Year	Out-turn Prices			November 1986 Prices		
	Attendance Allowance	Invalid Care Allow.	SB B&L (Indp't Homes)	Attendance Allowance	Invalid Care Allow.	SB B&L (Indp't Homes)
1976–7	£127 m	2	–	309	5	–
1977–8	167	3	–	369	6	–
1978–9	168	4	6	343	7	12
1979–80	203	4	10	352	7	17
1980–1	243	5	18	350	8	26
1981–2	332	6	23	425	8	29
1982–3	416	8	39	498	10	47
1983–4	495	10	105	562	11	119
1984–5	576	11	200	629	12	218
1985–6	686	84	333	706	87	343
1986–7	773	100	489	773	100	489

Sources: Attendance Allowance and Invalid Care Allowance – 1976–7 to 1984–5 from Appropriation Accounts, 1985–6 provisional outturn and 1986–7 published forecast (Cmnd 9789), as supplied by DHSS.

Invalid Care Allowance for 1985–6 and 1986–7 are study team estimates based on assumptions of 60,000 and 70,000 additional claimants due to the extension of the allowance to married women.

Supplementary Benefit, Board and Lodging (Independent Homes) – 1976–7 to 1984–5 are as provided by DHSS. Figures for 1985–6 and 1986–7 are the study team estimates described in Appendix D. All figures relate to the equivalent annual cost in early December within the financial year.

Expenditure at November 1986 prices is based on the revaluer to allow for Personal Social Services inflation with assumed inflation of 6% and 3% for 1985–6 and 1986–7 respectively.

EXHIBIT 15

CHANGES IN HOSPITAL STAFF AND PATIENT NUMBERS
England only. Mental Handicap and Mental Illness Hospitals and Units within other Hospitals

	Average Daily Occupied Beds		Nurse Numbers at 30 September wte's	
	MH	MI	MH	MI
1974	50,400	89,900	21,030	42,976
1975	49,600	86,900	23,224	47,259
1976	48,800	83,800	23,734	47,617
1977	47,900	80,800	24,515	49,433
1978	46,600	78,200	25,259	49,638
1979	45,400	76,500	25,774	50,305
1980	44,100	75,200	27,404	52,577
1981	43,000	73,400.	29,275	55,400
1982	41,600	71,300	29,809	56,799
1983	40,300	69,300	29,829	57,422
1984	38,600	67,000	30,039	57,555
1985	36,400	64,800	30,978	57,956

Source: Average daily occupied beds – DHSS Statistical Bulletin 2/86, Table 3.

Nurse Numbers – Mental Health Statistics for England 1984 Booklet 9 Table 7, and Booklet 10 Table 7. Earlier years provided by SR2C division, DHSS. Data for 1985 are provisional.

C – SOCIAL SECURITY BENEFITS

DOWNRATING OF BENEFITS IN INSTITUTIONAL CARE

1. A very wide range of social security benefits provide financial support for people living in the community. The purpose of this appendix is to describe some aspects of social security benefits that have particular relevance to community care.

2. State pensions, most contributory benefits (e.g. sickness benefit) and normal Supplementary Benefit payments, are downrated, or terminated, for those who enter long-stay public institutional care. The rules depend on the circumstances of the individual, and the type of institution into which they are admitted. Retirement pensions and contributory benefits are unaffected by entry to private and voluntary homes (except that they are treated as income for any person claiming Supplementary Benefits).

3. Those receiving state pensions or other contributory benefits have these downrated after eight weeks in hospital, with a further adjustment taking place after 52 weeks. A claimant with no dependents has the following reductions in entitlement:

(a) After eight weeks benefits are reduced by 40% of the basic retirement pension (i.e. by £15.50 per week)

(b) After 52 weeks, benefits are reduced to 20% of the basic retirement pension (i.e. to £7.75 per week, the 'hospital pocket money' rate).

4. However, the difference between rates (a) and (b) can be built up between weeks 53 and 104, and repaid as a Resettlement Benefit, if and when the claimant returns to the community. The Resettlement Benefit is normally paid weekly, in addition to other benefits, and at a rate equivalent to 160% of basic retirement pension (i.e. £62.00 per week). After 104 weeks in hospital, benefit continues at the hospital pocket money rate, but the amount repayable as a Resettlement Benefit does not increase.

5. A claimant with dependents, suffers a reduction in benefit of 20% of the basic retirement pension (i.e. reduced by £7.75 per week) after eight weeks in hospital. After 52 weeks their benefit is reduced to the hospital pocket money rate, but the balance of their entitlement can continue if it is signed over to their dependents. If claimants choose not to transfer the benefit to their dependents the amount foregone will accumulate towards a possible Resettlement Benefit under the rules described above.

6. Supplementary Benefit payments to people without dependents will normally cease on entry to hospital. Persons who have no other income, are normally entitled to Supplementary Benefit at the hospital pocket money rate (i.e. £7.75 per week), plus an amount for certain necessary continuing housing commitments. In December 1983, the latest date for which information is available, about 5,000 people were receiving Supplementary Benefit at the hospital pocket money rate. Approximately half of these were pensioners. No figures are available on total expenditure.

7. Residents in local authority homes pay for their accommodation in accordance with their means. The local authority fixes a standard charge based on the economic cost of a home place and residents pay as much of this as their resources permit. The rules for calculating how much a resident is able to pay, the minimum charge which the authority must levy (at present

£30.95 per week) and the amount residents must be allowed to retain for personal expenses (£7.75 per week) are all laid down centrally. If the resident has less income than the basic retirement pension (and savings of less than £3,000) they are entitled to Supplementary Benefits. The DHSS will assess their requirements as the minimum charge plus the allowance for personal expenses. Provisional figures for December 1984 indicate that there were 35,000 recipients of Supplementary Benefits in Part III accommodation. Figures on the cost of these payments are not available.

8. Against this background, the rest of this appendix describes in turn, each of the various allowances and benefits likely to affect mentally or physically handicapped, mentally ill or elderly people.

SUPPLEMENTARY BENEFIT – BOARD AND LODGING PAYMENTS

9. Supplementary Benefit for board and lodging is payable to the residents of private and voluntary homes, including registered nursing homes, and also to those placed in ordinary board and lodgings. Benefit is not payable if the claimant has capital over £3,000. For people in residential care and nursing homes the amount of benefit payable is the amount of their charge, (subject to maximum limits), plus an allowance for personal expenses, less their assessed income. Occupational pensions, state pensions, Severe Disablement Allowance and other contributory benefits are taken into account as income in full; the first £4.00 of net weekly earnings from part-time work, and the Mobility Allowance, are disregarded.

Residential Care Homes and Nursing Homes

10. The rules governing the payment of benefit for board and lodging have changed twice in the last three years in an attempt to regain control on rising expenditure. Prior to November 1983, each local office had one local limit covering all forms of board and lodging, but local DHSS offices had the discretionary power to pay the full amount of a board and lodging charge, provided it was not reasonable to expect the claimant to move to cheaper accommodation. During the early 1980's this discretionary power came to be more and more widely used.

11. In November 1983, new locally-determined limits were set for three categories of accommodation (ordinary board and lodgings, residential care homes and nursing homes), the limits being set at the 'highest reasonable charge' for suitable accommodation in the area. There was in addition, a further discretionary allowance (£16.15 in November 1984) for those with special care needs. Following further increases in the benefit expenditure the DHSS imposed a freeze on local limits in September 1984, and new arrangements were introduced in April 1985.

12. Under the new arrangements local limits were scrapped and the limits were now set centrally through regulations. The new national limits were set according to the type of home in which the claimant was resident, with no regional variation. Transitional arrangements were made for those currently receiving benefit in excess of the new limits. The weekly limits applying to residential care homes from November 1985 to July 1986 were as follows (the limits introduced in April 1985 being shown in brackets):

Physically Disabled (incurred below pension age)	£180 (£170)
Mentally Handicapped	£150 (£140)
Drug or Alcohol Dependent	£130 (£120)
Mentally Ill	£130 (£120)
Elderly or Other	£120 (£110)

The corresponding limits for registered nursing homes were £50 (£28.60) above these limits. People in hospices and other homes caring for the terminally ill could claim up to £230 (£198.60).

13. Further changes to the limits were made in July 1986, as follows:

- For those in residential care homes for the elderly and others, the limit was increased by £5.00 to £125 per week
- For those elderly people in residential care homes who would qualify for the higher rate Attendance Allowance, and for blind people over pension age, the limit was increased by £20 to £140 per week
- For those in residential care homes or nursing homes in Greater London, the limit was increased by a special extension of up to £17.50 per week.

The limits applying from July 1986 are as follows:

Table C – 1: BOARD AND LODGING ALLOWANCES
Private Residential Care or Nursing Homes
£ per week at July 1986

| | Outside of London | | Greater London | |
	Residential	Nursing	Residential	Nursing
Elderly and Other	£125 per week	170	142.50	187.50
Very Dependent Elderly or Blind Elderly	140	170	157.50	187.50
Mentally Ill or Drug/Alcohol Dependent	130	180	147.50	197.50
Mentally Handicapped	150	200	167.50	217.50
Physically Disabled below pension age	180	230	197.50	247.50
Terminally Ill	–	230	–	247.50

14. Residential care and nursing homes are required by law to be registered according to the client group for which they are catering. Residential care homes, having more than three residents, must be registered with the local authority (county, metropolitan district or London borough) and nursing homes must be registered with their district health authority. In setting registration standards, local authorities are guided by the *Home Life* code of practice, produced by a DHSS-sponsored working party under the chairmanship of Lady Avebury. Guidance on the registration standards for nursing homes is published by the National Association of Health Authorities. A home may be registered for more than one type of care, in which case the maximum amount of Supplementary Benefits payable will be determined by the adjudication officer of the DHSS according to the type of care being provided. Residents of unregistered homes with three or less residents can also claim up to the national limits if the adjudication officer is satisfied that they are providing the appropriate level of care.

15. Other changes in benefit levels were introduced in April 1985 with the national limits. Those claimants in receipt of an Attendance Allowance now have this included as income if they are resident in a residential or nursing home, and the level of personal allowance (payable in addition to the board and lodging allowance, to buy clothes and to cover other personal expenses) was reduced from £10.30 to £8.50 (£9.05 from July 1986).

16. The numbers of claimants in independent homes was estimated to be 42,000 at December 1984 with an estimated expenditure of £200 million. The corresponding figures for the years 1978 to 1984 are presented in Table C – 2.

Table C – 2: SUPPLEMENTARY BENEFIT BOARD AND LODGING PAYMENTS
Residents in Private and Voluntary Homes. Great Britain

	Beneficiaries	Annual Cost	Average Weekly Payment
1978	7,000	£ 6 million	£15.70 per week
1979	11,000	10	18.00
1980	12,000	18	28.10
1981	12,000	23	36.20
1982	15,700	39	47.70
1983	26,400	105	76.30
1984 (provisional)	42,000	200	91.50

Ordinary Board and Lodging and Hostels

17. Many people in the priority groups live in ordinary board and lodging accommodation and hostels. These may claim Supplementary Benefits for their board and lodging charges up to certain limits.

18. Throughout the country, board and lodging areas have been established and limits have been set ranging between £45 and £70 for what can be paid on top of the personal expenses allowance (£9.80 short-term, £10.95 long-term) to people in ordinary board and lodging accommodation. The limit for hostels is £70 nationally. Claimants over pension age or who are infirm may also be eligible for the extension (£17.50 from July 1986) to these limits.

19. Provisional figures for December 1984 indicate 163,000 claimants in ordinary board and lodging and hostels and an equivalent annual cost of over £500 million. Although this covers a variety of claimants including physically and mentally handicapped and elderly people, over 70% of the 1984 total boarders were claiming because they were unemployed. Provisional figures indicate that 39% of the total were aged 16–25, and 90% of this younger group were claiming as unemployed. Table C – 3 presents Supplementary Benefit expenditure and the numbers of beneficiaries in ordinary board and lodging from 1979 to 1984.

Table C – 3: SUPPLEMENTARY BENEFIT BOARD AND LODGING PAYMENTS
Claimants in Ordinary Board and Lodging Great Britain

	Beneficiaries	Annual Cost	Average Weekly Payment
1979	49,000	£ 52 million	£20.40 per week
1980	55,000	76	26.60
1981	69,000	115	32.15
1982	85,000	166	37.80
1983	112,000	278	47.70
1984 (provisional)	163,000	503	59.30

Data in Tables C – 2 and C – 3 are taken from the *Annual Statistical Enquiry* showing the position at December of each year. 1984 figures are provisional. Average benefit figures include the personal expenses allowance, but are net of other income, such as retirement pension, which fails to be taken into account in the Supplementary Benefit assessment. The trend in benefit payments does not therefore give an accurate reflection of the movement in charges: it indicates only the movement in that part of the charge that it fell to Supplementary Benefits to meet.

MOBILITY ALLOWANCE

20. The main conditions of entitlement for the Mobility Allowance are:
  (i) Inability or virtual inability to walk due to physical disablement.
  (ii) Beneficiaries must be aged five or over, and must satisfy conditions of entitlement before their 65th birthday. Benefit can continue in payment up to age 75.
  (iii) Beneficiaries must be able to benefit from enhanced facilities for locomotion (e.g. not in a coma, nor unable to be moved for medical reasons).

21. This allowance is payable regardless of the financial circumstances of the beneficiary, and regardless of any other benefits or support to which he is entitled. There is no downrating for those in hospital, nursing homes or residential accommodation. Further, it is not assessable for Income Tax, nor does it count towards any Supplementary Benefit entitlements. The rate applying from July 1986 is £21.65 per week. The number of beneficiaries and overall expenditure for the last three years is shown as follows in the 1986 Public Expenditure White Paper:

	Beneficiaries	Annual Cost
1983–4	315,000	£304 million
1984–5	355,000	356
1985–6	400,000	430

Many claimants will be receiving Mobility Allowance in addition to other benefits. In particular, Mobility Allowance entitlement satisfies the disablement requirements for the Severe Disablement Allowance.

22. The Oglesby Review in 1983 (ref. 50) looked at the problems of Mobility Allowance accumulating for hospital in-patients who have no prospect of spending it. Alternative solutions proposed were the downrating or freezing of payments once the accrued amount was equivalent to one year's payments, or to allow health authorities to spend the money for the benefit of all patients. As yet, a decision has not been taken on the implementation of this recommendation.

SEVERE DISABLEMENT ALLOWANCE

23. The Severe Disablement Allowance (SDA) was introduced in November 1984, and replaced the Non-Contributory Invalidity Pension (NCIP). The main conditions of entitlement are:

(i) Incapacity for work. (The incapacity must have already continued for 196 consecutive days).

(ii) In addition those whose incapacity for work begins after their 20th birthday must also be 80% disabled.

(iii) Beneficiaries must be 16 or over, and must qualify for SDA before reaching pension age. They can continue to receive SDA if their SDA allowance exceeds their entitlement to retirement pension.

(iv) Hospital downrating after eight weeks. This applies to hospitals and other institutions where the cost is being borne out of public or local funds.

The allowance is payable regardless of the financial circumstances of the beneficiary.

24. The rate of the SDA applying from July 1986 is £23.25 per week. The number of beneficiaries of the SDA and the NCIP for the last three years, together with the overall cost, is as follows:

	Beneficiaries		Annual Cost
	NCIP	SDA	
1983–4	210,000	–	£182 million
1984–5	225,000	245,000	232
1985–6	–	230,000	228

The number of beneficiaries of NCIP and SDA in 1984–5 are based on the averages for the periods April–November and November–March respectively. The apparent drop in beneficiaries, and the consequent cost for 1985–6, results from a change in the basis upon which the estimates were derived. There is no evidence of an actual fall in the number of beneficiaries.

ATTENDANCE ALLOWANCE

25. Attendance Allowance is payable at one of two rates (see below) to people aged two and over who by virtue of mental or physical disablement are, and have been for at least six months before an award is made, in need of:

(i) Frequent attention throughout the day in connection with their bodily functions, or

(ii) Continual supervision throughout the day to avoid substantial danger to themselves or others.

(iii) Prolonged or repeated attention at night, or

(iv) Continual supervision at night to avoid substantial danger to themselves or others.

In the case of a child under 16 the attention or supervision has to be substantially in excess of that normally required by a child of the same age.

26. The higher rate £30.95 per week from July 1986, is payable to those who satisfy a day *and* night condition; the lower rate £20.65, is payable to those satisfying either the day *or* night condition.

27. The allowance is not payable in hospital or residential accommodation, the cost of which is borne out of public or local funds, with the exception of the first four weeks in hospital or other accommodation. Thereafter a break at home of 29 days has to be made before a further 4 weeks is payable in accommodation. The allowance *can* be payable in privately run nursing and residential homes or half-way houses *but* only if the costs of accommodation are not being met out of public or local funds – whether wholly or in part. Payment is also precluded if the cost *may* be met out of public funds. This is applied particularly where a local authority had in the past met the cost of accommodation but then ceases to do so. The allowance remains not payable except for the first four weeks as in the previous paragraph.

28. The underlying principle is that the allowance is for people being cared for at home. It is not therefore payable in accommodation paid for out of public funds to avoid duplicate provision. For these purposes Supplementary Benefit is not public funds.

29. At March 1985, there were an estimated 543,000 beneficiaries, compared with 469,000 in March 1984. Approximately 40% of beneficiaries are under the age of 65; about 41% claim at the higher rate. Expenditure in 1984–5 was £576 million; £686 million in 1985–6. (See also Exhibit 11).

INVALID CARE ALLOWANCE

30. The Invalid Care Allowance is for those who give up work to care for an invalid. The main conditions of entitlement are:
   (i) Beneficiaries must be caring for someone, who is in receipt of the Attendance Allowance or Constant Attendance Allowance, for at least 35 hours per week.
   (ii) Beneficiaries must be between 16 and retirement age. (Until a recent case was brought before the European Court married women were ineligible).
   (iii) Earnings of beneficiaries must not exceed £12 per week.

31. The allowance is non-contributory and is not means-tested. It counts as income for the purposes of Income Tax and Supplementary Benefit entitlement. It does not affect the invalid's entitlement to Attendance Allowance, and continues payable for up to four weeks if the invalid goes into hospital or other accommodation. Should the *carer* go into hospital, the Invalid Care Allowance may stop immediately, or may go on for up to 12 weeks, depending on the circumstances of the carer and those of the disabled person being cared for during the six months before the carer goes into hospital.

32. The allowance applying from July 1986 is £23.25 per week, with additions for a wife and each child. The number of claimants and the overall expenditure for the last three years is as follows:

	Beneficiaries	Annual Cost
1983–4	8,800	£11 million
1984–5	9,500	11
1985–6	10,500	13

However these estimates do not take account of the extension of the allowance to married women, backdated to December 1984. It is estimated that this will lead to 70,000 additional beneficiaries in a full year.

HOUSING BENEFIT

33. There are two types of Housing Benefit (HB), Certificated, and Standard. The rules are as follows:

Certificated Housing Benefit – payable to people receiving Supplementary Benefits. The DHSS issues a certificate to the local authority authorising 100% help with claimant's rent and/or rates (less any deductions for a non-dependent in the household as for ineligible items such as charges for fuel included in the rent).

Standard Housing Benefit – payable to people not on Supplementary Benefit but who are eligible under a separate means test for help with their rent and/or rates. This includes the rent element of the charge paid by people in independent homes. The amount of benefit payable depends firstly upon the amount by which the claimant's gross income, less specified disregards, is above or below the HB 'needs allowance'. Until the uprating which took effect during week commencing 28 July 1986, the needs allowance was based on the appropriate long-term Supplementary Benefit scale rate for a single householder/couple, plus 40% of average local authority rents, plus 40% of average domestic rates plus 100% of average water/sewerage charges. For a number of reasons, this formula could not be followed in July 1986, so existing basic needs allowances were increased by the same cash increase as state retirement pensions. Additional amounts are added for each dependent child, where the claimant or his wife are pensioners or where one or both of them are handicapped. A single parent has the benefit of being allocated the same needs allowance as a couple.

- Where income *equals* the claimant's needs allowance, benefit equal to 60% of eligible rent and rates is paid
- Where income is *greater* than the needs allowance, 'tapers' of 29% for rent and 13% rates are applied (i.e. for each £1 of income in excess, the 60% rebate or allowance figure is reduced by 29p or 13p). Thus the higher the income the lower the benefit
- Where income is *less* than the needs allowance, the 60% rebate or allowance figure is increased by as follows:

    For non pensioners rent 25p, rates 8p, for each pound
    For pensioners rent 50p, rates 20p, for each pound.

    The smaller the income the larger the benefit up to 100% of eligible rent and/or rates.

34. *Housing Benefit Supplement* is a Supplementary Benefit payment for certain recipients of Standard Housing Benefit. It ensures that a person has no less income on which to live after paying rent and rates (reduced by standard HB) than he would have had if he had been entitled to normal Supplementary Benefit. For administrative convenience it is paid by the local authority together with Standard Housing Benefit. As it is technically a payment of Supplementary Benefit it carries with it entitlement to various other benefits such as free optical and dental treatment. The latest figures available for Housing Benefit Supplements are for 1983–4 and are 228,000 recipients at an annual cost of £29 million.

35. The estimated number of households in receipt of Certificated Housing Benefit, and the associated overall cost (rent and rate rebates, rent allowances) since the current scheme was introduced in 1983 are as follows:

	Households	Annual Cost
1983–4	3,650,000	£2.35 billion
1984–5	3,500,000	2.71
1985–6	3,560,000	2.98
1986–7	3,570,000	2.94

36. The equivalent figures for Standard Housing Benefit are as follows:

	Households	Annual Cost
1983–4	3,880,000	£1.38 billion
1984–5	3,790,000	1.49
1985–6	3,700,000	1.61
1986–7	3,330,000	1.60

(Source: 1986 Public Expenditure White Paper)

37. In Autumn 1983 the total number of households, by type of tenure and type of household was as shown in Table C – 4 below:

Table C – 4: ANALYSIS OF HOUSING BENEFIT RECIPIENTS
Autumn 1983 000's Households. Great Britain

	Standard	Certificated	Total
Total Households	3,990	2,980	6,970
Home Owners	1,590	620	2,210
Council Tenants	1,910	1,820	3,720
Other	490	540	1,040
Pensioners	2,690	1,440	4,130
Families with Children	650	850	1,500
Other	680	690	1,370

No records are kept of any other client group. It is not therefore possible to identify how many Housing Benefit recipients are, for example, mentally ill or physically handicapped people.

38. Residents of independent residential and nursing homes, who are not receiving a board and lodging allowance, may be entitled to Housing Benefit on the rental element of charges, less deductions for water charges and amenities. The rental element also excludes board, medical and nursing costs. From 28 July 1986, residents of local authority Part III homes (or in independent homes where they are sponsored by local authorities under Part III arrangements) are no longer eligible to claim Housing Benefit. There are currently no figures available on the numbers of claimants and the cost of Housing Benefit payments to those in independent homes.

RATE RELIEF FOR DISABLED PERSONS

39. Under the Rating (Disabled Persons) Act 1978, ratepayers are entitled to claim rate relief for certain facilities essential to the well-being of disabled residents. The rate relief entitlement is 90% reimbursed by the DOE as a specific grant (outside of the Aggregate Exchequer Grant). The 10% balance is picked up by the rating authority and is taken into account when the block grant is calculated. The definition of disabled is very wide and includes all forms of substantial and permanent physical or mental disability.

40. Domestic ratepayers are entitled to relief on, for example, a specific room used by a disabled member of the household, an additional toilet required by a disabled member, or a garage used for a disabled person's car. The relief allowance is based on a prescribed rateable value for each type of facility which is multiplied by the local rate poundage.

41. Institutions catering for the disabled can have up to 100% relief entitlement on their rates. It is up to the local authority to determine the proportionate relief, for example if the institution contains accommodation

for the proprietor or otherwise not used exclusively to provide facilities for disabled people. The institutions covered can include local authority, private and voluntary homes, training centres and special schools.

The total specific grant expenditure in 1984–5 was £55 million, made up as follows:

	Recipients	Average Entitlement Total
Domestic	89,000	£ 84
Institutions	13,500	3,400

* * *

The types of allowances that are available to support those in community or hospital care, are summarised in Table C–5. The number of claimants and the associated annual cost include all client groups in receipt of the benefit. This table excludes normal Supplementary Benefits that are available to those living in their own homes. If nothing else this appendix and the summary table show how very confused and complex the present arrangements have become.

Table C – 5: SUMMARY OF ALLOWANCES, 1984–5

Allowance	Accommodation in which it is payable					Weekly Limit	Personal Expenses	Claimants (000's)	Annual Cost
	Means Tested	Own Home	LA Pt III	NHS Hosp-ital	P & V Home or Lodgings				
Supplementary Benefit B & L (Independent homes)	Yes	No	No	No	Yes	£125 – 247.50	£ 9.05	42[1]	£ 200 m[1]
Supplementary Benefit B & L (Ordinary)	Yes	No	No	No	Yes	45 – 70	9.80 or 10.95	163[1]	503[1]
Supplementary Benefit (Part III)	Yes	No	Yes	No	No	30.95	7.75	35[1]	N/A
Mobility Allowance	No	Yes	Yes	Yes	Yes	21.40	–	355	356
Severe Disablement Allowance	No	Yes	Yes[2]	Yes[2]	Yes[2]	23.00[3]	–	245	232
Attendance Allowance	No	Yes	No	No	Yes[4]	20.45 or 30.60	–	469	576
Invalid Care Allowance	No	Yes[5]	No	No	No	23.00[3]	–	10	13
Housing Benefit	Yes	Yes	No[6]	No	Yes[7]	N/A	–	7,300	4,200
Rate Relief for Disabled	No	Yes	Yes	No	Yes	N/A	–	102	61

NOTES

1. These are provisional figures at December 1984.
2. SDA is treated as income in assessing SB payments. It is downrated after eight weeks in hospital, or immediately if the claimant moves directly into hospital from Part III accommodation.
3. With additions for a wife and dependent children.
4. Attendance Allowance is only payable if none of the accommodation cost is being met by a local authority. It is treated as income in assessing Supplementary Benefit board and lodging payments to people in residential and nursing homes, but not for those in ordinary board and lodging.
5. Invalid Care Allowance is treated as income if the provider of care is receiving Supplementary Benefit.
6. Housing Benefit could be claimed in Part III accommodation up until July 1986.
7. Housing Benefit is payable on the rental element of charges less any deduction for non-eligible items, if the claimant is not in receipt of Supplementary Benefit board and lodging payments.

D – SURVEY OF PRIVATE AND VOLUNTARY HOMES AND SUPPLEMENTARY BENEFIT EXPENDITURE

1. A major factor in the provision of services for the priority groups has been the rapid rise in the number of places in Private and Voluntary (P&V) homes. Furthermore, whilst the number of P&V residents has been increasing the number of them who are being financially supported by local authorities has fallen sharply. Together these two trends have serious implications for Supplementary Benefit payments of board and lodging.

2. The most recent published figures on P&V homes and local authority supported residents in England, relate to March 1984 for elderly and younger physically handicapped people and to March 1983 for the mentally ill and mentally handicapped people. Figures for March 1985 became available during the course of the study in unpublished form, but were not due to be published before November 1986. In view of this, and because many authorities reported an increased pace of change over the last two years, the Audit Commission sent out a questionnaire to all directors of social services in England and Wales, requesting certain summary data. The data requested related to P&V residential homes within the local authority's area, for March 1985 and March 1986, and was as follows:
   - The total number of residents in homes for elderly and younger physically handicapped people, aged under 65, and aged 65 and over
   - The total number of adult and junior places in homes for mentally handicapped people
   - The total number of places in homes for mentally ill people.

3. March 1984 figures were provided to the local authority for validation. In addition, authorities were asked to provide copies of their returns to the DHSS for 1985 and 1986, showing the number of supported residents in different client groups. In all, 84% of authorities (97 out of 116) responded, although not all were able to provide every item of data requested. In fact only 54% of all authorities were able to provide complete information on the supported residents at March 1986.

RESULTS

4. The main results of the survey are summarised in Tables D – 1 and D – 2, which show the total for England and Wales once the returns have been grossed up to allow for the authorities that did not respond. The main conclusions are as follows:
   (i) The total number of residents in P&V homes has increased by approximately 15,000 in each of the last two years.
   (ii) The number of physically disabled residents has remained broadly constant, the number of elderly has increased linearly and the growth in places for the mentally ill and mentally handicapped has accelerated during 1985–6.
   (iii) The number of residents in all client groups, who are supported by local authorities has fallen dramatically since 1985. In March 1986 there were little over half the number of supported residents that there had been two years previously.
   (iv) There is a marked imbalance between the situation in London and

elsewhere. Over the two year period the number of P&V residents in London has increased by only 8% whereas elsewhere it has increased by 33%. Similarly, the number of local authority supported residents in such homes has fallen by 27% in London and by 52% elsewhere. Nearly one half of all local authority supported residents in England and Wales are now in homes within London. It remains to be seen how much of these imbalances will be corrected by the special extension to Supplementary Benefit board and lodging limits for Greater London, which was introduced in July 1986.

Table D – 1:   RESIDENTS OF PRIVATE VOLUNTARY RESIDENTIAL HOMES FOR ELDERLY AND YOUNGER PHYSICALLY HANDICAPPED PEOPLE

	Aged under 65			Aged 65 and over		
	March 1984	March 1985	March 1986	March 1984	March 1985	March 1986
Total Residents						
London	971	986	1,020	9,037	9,609	9,728
Met Districts	1,239	988	1,088	10,446	13,361	15,903
English Counties	6,325	6,825	6,480	59,194	68,826	79,013
Wales	271	313	298	3,220	4,044	4,963
Total	8,806	9,112	8,886	81,899	95,841	109,607
Annual Change		+3.5%	−2.5%		+17.0%	+14.4%
Numbers Supported by Local Authorities						
London	788	767	585	4,136	3,348	2,738
Met Districts	844	873	461	1,676	1,244	604
English Counties	2,269	2,094	1,346	4,495	3,031	1,134
Wales	201	156	104	318	220	56
Total	4,102	3,891	2,496	10,625	7,843	4,532
Annual Change		−5.1%	−35.8%		−26.2%	−42.2%

Table D – 2:   PRIVATE AND VOLUNTARY HOMES FOR MENTALLY ILL AND MENTALLY HANDICAPPED PEOPLE

	March 1984	March 1985	March 1986
Total Places in Registered Homes			
London	1,139	1,242	1,256
Met Districts	1,076	1,478	1,707
English Counties	6,614	6,578	8,194
Wales	673	734	760
Total	9,502	10,032	11,917
Annual Change		+5.6%	+18.8%
Numbers Supported by Local Authorities			
London	2,465	2,319	2,035
Met Districts	858	735	493
English Counties	2,876	2,566	2,170
Wales	175	277	159
Total	6,374	5,897	4,856
Annual Change		−7.5%	−17.6%

5. The results for March 1985 are broadly consistent with unpublished data available from DHSS and the Welsh Office.

The comparison is as follows:

	Survey	DHSS and Welsh Office Data
Places in Registered Homes		
Residents under 65	9,112	8,778
Residents 65 and over	95,841	96,006
Places for Mentally Ill and Handicapped People	10,032	10,267
Numbers supported by Local Authorities		
Aged under 65	3,891	3,875
Aged 65 and over	7,843	8,734
Mentally Ill and Mentally Handicapped	5,897	6,026

6. There are two reasons for the small discrepancies that have occurred. Firstly, the DHSS use a gazetteer system for P&V residential homes; this means that the previous year's data can be used in respect of homes that make no return in a particular year. There is a danger that the Commission's once-off estimates will omit some homes that failed to make a return. Secondly, in answering the questionnaire, at least two authorities discovered errors (of 78 and 524 residents) in figures that they had previously supplied to the DHSS. In the analysis that follows the DHSS and Welsh Office data for March 1985 (corrected for the above errors) have been adopted. The survey has been used to determine the percentage changes for the year to March 1986.

DISTRIBUTION OF SUPPLEMENTARY BENEFIT BOARD AND LODGING EXPENDITURE

7. A Special Statistical Exercise by the DHSS for the period 29 April to 29 July 1985 provides the only available data on the distribution of Supplementary Benefit payments for board and lodging (Independent Homes) claims by category of care. The percentage of all cases by different categories of care is shown in Table D – 3 below. This excludes the 5% of Scottish cases and allocates pro rata the 7% of cases that were not defined according to category of care.

Table D – 3: ANALYSIS OF SUPPLEMENTARY BENEFIT CLAIMS, 1985
% Cases

Category of Home	Residential Care	Nursing Home
Elderly (inc. general nursing home)	69.8%	14.6
Mentally Infirm	3.6	0.3
Alcohol and Drug Dependency	0.7	0.1
Mentally Handicapped	5.9	0.1
Physically Disabled	1.2	0.2
Other	3.0	–
Hospices	–	0.5
Total	84.2	15.8

8. The same statistical exercise also gave information on the distribution of claims by social security regions. Unfortunately the social security regions are too large to indicate detailed variation between localities. Nevertheless, the data does indicate that the pattern of claims broadly reflects the total numbers of places available. As Table D – 4 shows, only London North has significantly below and North Western region significantly above the average proportion of P&V residents claiming board and lodging payments.

Table D – 4: REGIONAL ANALYSIS OF P&V RESIDENTIAL HOMES FOR THE ELDERLY
Spring 1985. Residents and Beneficiaries per 1000 people aged 75+

Social Security Region	Total Elderly Residents	SB Beneficiaries	% Residents receiving SB
North Eastern	20.5/1000	7.0	34%
Midlands	21.9	7.4	34
London North	25.2	5.1	20
London South	38.8	12.8	33
Wales & S Western	40.1	13.3	33
North Western	27.9	11.8	42

Note. The total number of elderly residents is based on the DHSS 'RA3 returns' for 31 March 1985. The number of SB beneficiaries includes only those in residential homes for the elderly. It excludes those in 'Other' Residential Homes and those not identified by category of care. It includes all new and repeat claims during a three month period and so does not represent a precise picture at a single point in time. Thus the figures can be taken as broad estimates only.

ESTIMATE OF THE CURRENT NUMBER OF B & L CLAIMS

9. The most recent published data on the total number of Supplementary Benefit Board and Lodging (Independent Homes) claims are provisional figures for December 1984. These showed 42,000 beneficiaries in Great Britain at an equivalent annual cost £200 million. This represented an increase of 170% in beneficiaries, and of 400% in expenditure, over the figures for December 1982.

10. The results of the Commission's survey have been used to estimate the number of beneficiaries during a single week in December 1985 and December 1986. Table D – 5 below presents the full list of data used by the study team.

Table D – 5: INPUT DATA USED BY THE STUDY TEAM
At March 31

	1982	1983	1984	1985	1986
Number of Elderly and Younger Physically Handicapped (YPH) Residents of Private and Voluntary Homes:					
1. England < 65	7,703	8,368	8,592	8,494	8,282
2. England 65+	61,955	68,610	78,547	91,515	104,693
3. Wales < 65	243	215	271	316	308
4. Wales 65+	2,101	2,460	3,220	4,045	4,628
Places in Private and Voluntary Residential Homes for Mentally Handicapped (MH) and Mentally Ill (MI) people:					
5. England MH	4,600	5,046	6,271	7,096	8,430
6. England MI	2,300	2,367	2,558	3,171	3,767
7. Wales MH & MI	513	624	673	734	872
Number of Residents in Private and Voluntary Homes Supported (financially) by Local Authorities:					
8. England < 65	4,160	4,053	3,901	3,708	2,381
9. England 65+	13,177	11,940	10,307	8,479	4,901
10. Wales < 65	229	197	201	167	107
11. Wales 65+	348	379	318	255	147
12. England MH	4,390	4,591	4,877	4,639	3,852
13. England MI	1,632	1,469	1,322	1,237	1,020
14. Wales MH & MI	181	181	181	162	133
SB B&L (Independent Homes) Claimants at 1 December:					
15. GB Total	15,700	26,427	42,000		

11. The sources of data for each line of the table are shown below.

Lines 1 & 2	1982–5: Health and Personal Social Services Statistics (HPSSS) for England 1986, Table 7.2. Figures for 1984 and 1985 have been adjusted for errors in two authorities' data, see paragraph 6 above. 1986: Study team forecast of growth (−2.5%, +14.4%), see Table D – 1 above.
Lines 3 & 4	1982–4: HPSSS for Wales 1985, Table 7.04. 1985: Residential Accommodation for the Elderly, Younger Physically Handicapped and Blind: Year ended March 31, 1985, Tables 2.1, 2.2 and 2.3. 1986: As lines 1 & 2 above. (Note that these figures differ from those in Table D – 1 in that the average surveyed growth across the whole of England and Wales has been applied to the Welsh Office data for March 1985).
Lines 5 & 6	1982–5: HPSSS for England 1986, Table 7.3. 1982 estimated by straight line interpolation. 1986: Study team forecast of growth (+18.8%) see Table D – 2 above.
Line 7	1982–4: HPSSS for Wales 1985, Table 7.05. 1985: Activities of SSD's: Year Ended March 31, 1985, Table 2.5 1986: As lines 5 & 6 above.
Lines 8 & 9	1982–5: HPSSS for England 1986, Table 7.1 1986: Study team forecast of change (−35.8%, −42.2%) see Table D – 1 above.
Lines 10 & 11	1982–4: HPSSS for Wales 1985, Table 7.01 1985: Activities of SSDs: Year Ended March 31, 1985, Table 1.1 1986: As lines 8 & 9 Above.
Lines 12 & 13	1982–3: DHSS Local Authority Statistics A/F83/11, Table 8 & Table 3. 1984–5: Special tabulations from SR6 division, DHSS. 1986: Study team forecast of change (−17.6%) see Table D – 2 above.
Line 14	1982–3: Value for 1984 adopted 1984: Activities of SSDs: Year Ended 31/3/84, Table 2.2 less Table 2.1. 1985: Activities of SSDs: Year Ended 31/3/85, Table 2.2 less Table 2.1. 1986: As lines 12 & 13 above.
Line 15	Figures provided by DHSS

12. The calculations involved in arriving at the study team estimates are set out in Table D – 6 below.

Table D – 6: STUDY TEAM ESTIMATES OF PUBLICLY SUPPORTED RESIDENTS IN PRIVATE AND VOLUNTARY HOMES
England and Wales

	1982	1983	1984	1985	1986
Residents in Residential Homes at *31 March*					
16. Elderly and YPH	72,000	79,700	90,600	104,400	117,900
of which:					
17. LA-Supported	17,900	16,600	14,700	12,600	7,500
18. SB or Unsupported	54,100	63,100	75,900	91,800	110,400
19. Mentally Handicapped/Ill	6,500	7,100	8,400	9,700	11,500
of which:					
20. LA-Supported	6,200	6,200	6,400	6,000	5,000
21. SB-Supported	300	800	2,000	3,600	6,500
SB–Supported and Unsupported Residents in Residential Homes at *1 December*					
22. Mentally Handicapped/Ill	700	1,600	3,100	5,500	8,400
23. Elderly and YPH	60,100	71,600	86,500	104,200	122,800
of which:					
24. Unsupported	48,200	52,100	56,000	59,900	63,800
25. SB-Supported	11,900	19,500	30,400	44,200	58,900
26. All clients SB-Supported	12,500	21,100	33,500	49,800	67,300
SB-Supported Residents in Residential and Nursing Homes at *1 December*					
27. England & Wales	14,900	25,100	39,900	59,200	80,200

Though the numbers are presented in Table D – 6 to the nearest 100 residents, the calculations have been performed to a greater degree of accuracy. Numbers do not necessarily add exactly, due to rounding.

13. The assumptions made, and the derivation of each line of the table, are set out below.

Line 16   Summation of lines 1 to 4 in Table D – 5.

Line 17   Summation of lines 8 to 11 to Table D – 5.

Line 18   All those residents of P&V residential homes for elderly and younger physically handicapped people, who are not financially supported by local authorities are either supported through SB board and lodging payments or are 'unsupported', i.e. line 16 minus line 17.

Line 19   It is assumed that 88% of places P&V residential homes for the mentally ill and mentally handicapped people, are occupied at any specific date. Thus, line 19 is the summation of lines 5 to 7 (Table D – 5) multiplied by 0.88.

Line 20   Summation of lines 12 to 14 in Table D – 5.

Line 21   It is assumed that all residents in P&V residential homes for mentally ill and mentally handicapped people are supported financially either by a local authority or through SB board and lodging payments. Thus line 21 is line 19 minus line 20. This assumption is necessary because inconsistencies arise if the percentage of SB beneficiaries who were in homes for mentally handicapped or mentally ill people in April to July 1985 (see paragraph 7), is adopted for earlier years.

Lines 22 & 23	The number of P&V residents who are supported by SB, or who are 'unsupported', at the beginning of December each year, is determined by straight line interpolation between the figures for 31 March in the same and following year. (Thus line 23 for 1982 comprises one-third of line 18 for 1982, and two-thirds of line 18 for 1983).
	The numbers for December 1986 are obtained by straight line extrapolation of the trend between March 1985 and March 1986. (Thus line 23 for 1986 is five-thirds of line 18 for 1986 minus two-thirds of line 18 for 1985).
Line 24	It is assumed that 5% of SB board and lodging beneficiaries in Great Britain are in homes in Scotland, and that of the remainder 16% are in nursing homes. These figures are based on the Special Statistical Exercise referred to in paragraph 8. Thus for years 1982 to 1984, line 24 is line 23 minus the difference between line 15 x 0.798 and line 22.
	The number of 'unsupported' residents derived in this way is found to be increasing annually, but to have fallen as a percentage of total residents in P&V homes for elderly and younger physically handicapped people (from 67% in 1982 to 62% in 1984). At least for the years 1982 to 1984, the increase in numbers appears to have been linear, an increase of 3,900 per annum. This linear trend has been assumed to continue through until 1986.
Line 25	The number of SB board and lodging beneficiaries in residential homes for elderly and younger physically handicapped people is obtained by subtracting from those not supported by local authorities (line 23) those who are unsupported (line 24).
Line 26	The total number of people in residential homes who are supported through SB board and lodging payments is obtained by adding the number in homes for mentally handicapped and mentally ill people (line 22) to the number in other homes (line 25).
Line 27	It is assumed that 16% of beneficiaries in England and Wales are in registered nursing homes (as in line 24). Thus line 27 is line 26 divided by 0.84.

ESTIMATE OF THE AVERAGE COST PER CLAIMANT

14. The most recent estimate of the average cost per claimant is £91.50 per week, at December 1984. This was before the introduction of national limits. In the absence of information to the contrary the team assumed that the introduction of national limits at April 1985 had a neutral effect on the average cost per claim. Because local limits had been frozen from September 1984 to April 1985 the team assumed that the average cost at December 1984 applied also (at prevailing prices) until the national limits were uprated in November 1985. This in fact would represent a dramatic turnaround from the previous situation where the cost per claim had virtually doubled over the previous two years.

15. The increased average cost per claim resulting from the revisions to the national limits at November 1985 and July 1986 have been estimated as follows:

    (i) The notional average weekly cost by type of home has been estimated by adding the personal allowance to the appropriate national limit and subtracting the single person's full retirement pension applying at the appropriate time (in practice many people will claim more and many less than this notional average).

    (ii) The average notional cost across all homes is estimated by applying the proportions by category of care determined by the special statistical exercise referred to above.

    (iii) This average notional cost is increased by 1% to 'normalise' it to the December 1984 figure (assumed to apply also in April 1985).

    (iv) In determining the average cost from July 1986 it is assumed that one-third of those in residential homes for elderly and other people are eligible for the new higher rate of £140 per week, and that 8% of claims are eligible for the Greater London supplement of £17.50 per week.

16. In practice the increased cost per claim resulting from a change in the national limits would not occur immediately, but there would be a time lag. However, the effect of this time lag on average costs at December of each year is likely to be more than compensated for by the conservative assumption of constant average costs between December 1984 and November 1985.

17. The result of this analysis is that the average cost per claimant is estimated to have risen by 12.5% during 1985, and by a further 8% during 1986. The analysis is summarised in Table D – 7 below.

ESTIMATE OF CURRENT SB BOARD AND LODGING EXPENDITURE

18. To determine the overall expenditure in England and Wales on SB Board and Lodging (Independent Homes) the study team multiplied the number of beneficiaries (Table D – 6, line 27) by the average weekly cost per claim (Table D – 7) to give an average weekly cost at December 1985 and December 1986. These have been multiplied by 52 to give an equivalent annual figure at prevailing prices. On this basis, expenditure for England and Wales is estimated to have risen from £190 million at December 1984, to £316 million at December 1985 and to £465 million at December 1986. On the assumption that 95% of beneficiaries in Great Britain are in England and Wales, the equivalent figures for Great Britain from December 1982 are as follows:

	Annual Rate of Expenditure
December 1982	£ 39 million
December 1983	105
December 1984	200
December 1985	334
December 1986	489

These are illustrated in Exhibit 11 in the main text.

Table D – 7: ESTIMATE OF THE AVERAGE COST PER CLAIMANT

		April 1985	November 1985	July 1986
Retirement Pension		£ 35.80 p/w	38.30	38.70
Personal Allowance		8.50	8.95	9.05
Notional Cost by Category of Care				
Residential Homes				
Elderly & Other	72.8%	82.70	90.65	100.35
Mentally Ill, Alcohol, Drugs	4.3	92.70	100.65	100.35
Mentally Handicapped	5.9	112.70	120.65	120.35
Physically Handicapped	1.2	142.70	150.65	150.35
Nursing Homes				
Elderly & Other	14.6	111.30	140.65	140.35
Mentally Ill, Alchohol, Drugs	0.4	121.30	150.65	150.35
Mentally Handicapped	0.1	141.30	170.65	170.35
Physically Handicapped	0.7	171.30	200.65	200.35
Hospice				
Mean outside London	100.0	90.63	101.96	108.94
London Supplement (average over all claims)		–	–	1.40
Mean Notional Cost		90.63	101.96	110.34
Average 'Normalised' Cost		91.50	102.94	111.40
% Change			12.50%	8.22%

Printed for Her Majesty's Stationery Office by Linneys Colour Print
Dd239991. C50. 12/86. 50264